REFLECTIONS ON ECONOMY AND SOCIETY OF TRIPURA

Reflections on Economy and Society of Tripura

Amitabha Sinha
Kiransankar Chakraborty

AKANSHA PUBLISHING HOUSE
NEW DELHI • GUWAHATI • VISAKHAPATNAM

AKANSHA PUBLISHING HOUSE
4649-B/21,Ansari Road
Daryaganj, New Delhi-110002
Phones: 23268193, 09435116718
Email: ektabooks@yahoo.com
visit us: www.akanshapublishinghouse.com

Reflections on Economy and Society of Tripura

First Published 2010

ISBN 978-81-8370-231-7

PRINTED IN INDIA

Published by Akansha Publishing House, New Delhi-110002 and printed at **Harmain Offset Press**

Contents

Preface

The State of Tripura is one of the eight States of the Northeastern region (NER) of India in which include Assam, Arunachal Pradesh, Meghalaya, Mizoram, Manipur, Nagaland and Sikkim. This region has around 7 per cent of the total geographical area of the country but around 4 per cent of the population. In fact, around 60 per cent of the population of NER resides in Assam. As a result, in most of the All India studies, Assam is taken as a proper representative State of NER. This approach has both justification and limitation. The justification is in terms of the size of the population. Since a very small percentage of the total population of India reside in the remaining seven States is .02 per cent, it is argued that in an All-India study, an analysis of these states can safely be ignored. But the demographic perspective of socio-economic analysis leads to marginalisation of the remaining states in the domain of social studies. This limitation of demographic approach needs correction. This book is a small contribution in this direction.

The major justification of considering Tripura as the universe of the study is based on a criticism of the demographic approach around the essential methodological stance of recognizing context specificity of socio-economic analysis. This raises the inherent debate between the two approaches to social science research. One school believes that social knowledge should not confuse the trees for the forest. It is the overall trend and general pattern that is relevant to socio-economic analysis rather than specific particular information. The other school argues that the search for a general theory in socio-economic research is like the search for the Holy Grail or the search for mirages in the desert. Socio-economic knowledge cannot be independent of the context, this can be knowledge of the particular, and the sum total of the particulars may not add up to any general design.

The topics covered in this book vary to the point of confusion if one fails to note the main objective of the book. One objective is of course simply providing reliable data in the specific areas touched upon by the book. The second is to entice interested readers on researchable topics. The third is getting feedbacks on the analysis undertaken here for further improvement. We take joint responsibility for the views presented in this book.

We are greatly indebted to the various Departments of Tripura State Government for their active cooperation. We also express our indebtedness to Mr. M.P. Misra, Akansha Publishing House, New Delhi, for taking all pains for publishing this book.

Amitabha Sinha
Kiran Sankar Chakraborty

List of Tables

1

An Insight into Urbanisation and Urban Growth in Tripura

The increase in population during the last few decades has resulted in high density in the urban areas which has created subhuman living conditions in most of the big cities of our country. The uncontrolled and haphazard suburban sprawl has focussed the attention of the community on the 'living off' of the additional new population into well-planned new towns or cities. It cannot be denied that cities in the developing countries like India are quite eager for material progress. They have been compelled by the circumstances to optimise the use of all sources by judiciously balancing the budgets for developing the newly created urban pockets sprung up with the development of economic activities. The present discourse has four sections including the present one. Section two focuses on understanding urban units and its characteristics. Section three deals with the meaning of urban units according to census of India. Finally, growth of urban units in Tripura has been discussed in section four.

Understanding Urban Units

Urbanisation and urban growth has always been an area of interest for sociologists, geographers, political scientists, economists, historians etc. The social scientists are thus conceptualising the area according to their needs. As a result, no universally accepted theory of urbanisation has emerged.. It is also a fact that urbanisation continues to knock at the door of theory. Sociologists, geographers, political scientists and economists are bringing together a specialised theoretical proposition. Thus, a single definition of city or urban unit is not suitable for all purposes. Rather than contribute to an endless debate on the subject, it is more realistic to grant that there are numerous ways of viewing urban unit all of which are relevant to understand the complex problem. It can be defined in terms of political status, demographic attributes (size and/or density), economic variables (the dominance of non-agricultural occupations), socio-cultural patterns of behavior independent of sustenance activities and even psychological characteristics. Some of the definitions pose particular problems, but none of them is intrinsically either 'right' or 'wrong'.

To define urban population, the only consideration is the population living in urban places. To define urban places, the criterion of an incorporated status, seems unsatisfactory because it is determined arbitrarily and subject to fictitious changes. For a long time the criterion of population density has received attention principally because of rapid urbanisation. Population density is, however, of little value because it depends on the administrative boundaries of the urban place. The concept of 'population/area of land under use' has certain advantages, but a serious limitation is that it is very difficult to apply in the study of a large number of cases. The concept may be justified in principle, but its use raises several practical problems. Other two criteria are the population size of a place and the industrial composition of its population. In actual practice these two criteria are applied independently of one another.

From the demographic point of view the urban unit is best determined in terms of the size of the inhabited locality and the structure of its population. Many factors such as geographical, economic, historical, cultural etc., determine the size of the population and the character of inhabited localities. These factors, in turn, are reflected in the character of the communes, whether they are made up of one or many localities. An urban place is distinguished from a rural agglomeration by having a larger population and a considerable degree of division of labour in both industrial production and services. The degree of the division of labour, however, does not vary directly with the size of the population of a place in all cases. Due to inhabiting effects of patriarchal system on the expansion of productive forces, there are some places which have little division of labour. The differentiation of population through the development of industry can give an inhabited place and urban character. Other urban attributes like rapid communication, efficient transportation, higher education, the provision of adequate health care facilities, etc. act as other highly differentiated activities. The development of the economic structure of the population however, cannot alone give urban character to a place, specially in cases where that development is uniform and oriented toward a single activity. For instance, there are places with a very high percentage of non-agricultural population (mines, isolated factories etc.), which, nevertheless, lack the character and organisation of urban places, as a result of having too few inhabitants. Thus, the urban character of a place depends upon the concurrence of these two factors, the size of the population and its type of economic development.

The socio-economic criteria of urban character may include the following: -

1) From the administrative view-point, (a) whether the place is legally a city, town or urban commune and (b) whether it is a district or sub-district headquarters.

2) As far as communications are concerned, (a) whether the place is on a railroad or (b) connected by national highway.

3) From the economic view-point, whether the place have (a) manufacturing establishments, (b) wholesaling establishments and (c) banking establishments.

4) From the public health view-point, whether the place has (a) permanent sanitary facilities and installations, (b) drinking water facilities, (c) hospitals.

5) From the educational view-point, whether the place has (a) technical or a secondary school, (b) school for girls.

6) From the cultural view-point, whether there is a (a) theater, or (b) museum, or (c) cinema hall.

It appears from the studies that most of the places defined as urban by the two criteria have also most of the economic, social, educational, cultural and communication facilities common in the towns of the region. Thus, it is of value to define urban places in this way. Inclusion of more criteria, according to local condition may also be considered for meaningful purpose.

Meaning of Urban Units as per Census of India

The decennial data published by the Census Authority of India are the best source of data for the study of urban growth and urbanisation in India. It is an usual feature in the presentation of census data to maintain a line of division between 'Rural' and 'Urban' population. This rural-urban dichotomy is accepted all over the world and recognised by the administration as well. To quote from 1981 census, "One of the basic characteristic of the population obtained through the census is the rural and urban distribution of the people. The distinction between rural and urban is not always amenable to a single definition, which could be applicable to all countries or for that matter, even within the same country. Quite often it has been asserted that an urban area should be distinguished not merely on the basis of defined demographic characteristics but also on the basis of the level of infrastructure facilities, Ideally, it would be useful to define urban areas in terms of the level of infrastructure development and the availability of amenities in a given area but criteria based on such consideration have not been adopted in defining as urban area in India".

The definition of town in Indian censuses remained the same all through the decades 1901-51. According to the Census of India, 1901, town includes (a) every municipality of whatever size; (b) all civil lines not included within municipal limits;

(c) every other continuous collection of houses, permanently inhabitated by not less than 5,000 persons, which the Provincial Superintendent may decide to treat as a town for census purposes. Thus the primary consideration was the administrative set-up, not the size of its population in deciding whether a place was urban or not. Moreover, the Census Superintendents had the discretion to consider as a 'town' any place, irrespective of other factors.

Due to inherent weakness in the definition of 'town' and lack of uniformity in its applications, Census Commissioners in several census reports (1911, 1941) have criticised the matter.

In census 1951, Mr. Ashok Mitra, the Census Superintendent of West Bengal, had put forward a comprehensive definition of town which had subsequently been taken as the standard census definition at all India level. The Union Table A-IV gave an account of the towns classified by population with variation since 1901 (Khasnobis and Nath, 1994).

The following definition of urban area has been adopted from 1951 onwards:

a) All places with a municipality, corporation, cantonment board or notified town committee etc.

b) All other places which satisfy the following criteria;

   i) a minimum population of 5000.

   ii) at least 75 per cent of male working population engaged in non-agricultural pursuits, and

   iii) a density of population of at least 400 person per sq. km (1000 person per sq.mile)

In addition, some places not satisfying these conditions are also classified as urban if they have distinct urban characteristics. The marginal cases include major project colonies, areas of intensive industrial development, railway colonies, tourist centers etc. (Visaria, 1991). The criteria of at least 75 per cent of male working population engaged in non-agriculture pursuits (b. iii) had been a minor change in 1981 census. The revised requirement as per 1981 census, is that 75 per cent of the male working population should be" outside the primary sector (Krishnamurthy, 1984).

A new concept of identifying "standard urban areas" was also adopted in 1971 census on the basis of the following onwards:

i) That there should be a core town with a minimum population size of 50,000.

ii) That the contiguous areas made up of other urban as well as rural administrative should have close mutual socio-economic links with the core town, and

iii) That the probabilities are that the contiguous area in question will get fully urbanised in a period of 2 to 3 decades.

The urban population of each census year has been divided into different categories according to size of urban centres. Thus the urban centre are categorised into six categories.

Category

Class - I	1,00,000 and above
Class - II	50,000 – 99,000
Class - III	20,000 – 49,999
Class - IV	10,000 – 19,999
Class - V	5000 – 9999
Class - VI	below 5000

Growth of Urban Units in Tripura

The present section deals with urbanisation and urban growth in Tripura. In Tripura we find that there was only one urban agglomeration during the first decades of the last century i.e. Agartala. There had been a considerable increase in the growth of total population during these decades (1.73 lakh in 1901 to 6.39 lakh in 1951) yet we find that this increase was well accommodated in the rural areas. There was no phenomenal urban growth because inter-country migration was the major contributing factor to this population spurt. Since they belonged essentially to cultivating stock, they flocked to the countryside, scrambled for agriculture land and settled as cultivators or landless labourer. Moreover, lack of industries or any other scope of employment deterred them from getting urbanised. The administrative headquarters was situated at Agartala, hence the only town or urban centre.

During the 1961 census the sub-divisional towns emerged and the total numbers increased to six. The reasons attributed to this may be the fact that sub-divisional towns were growing as district headquarters facilitating administrative reorganisation, communications developed though there were no railways connecting the entire State, the national highway was being extended till the extreme south, from the north. Peculiarity in Tripura's case was noticed when it was seen that refugee rehabilitation scheme helped in constructing the roads, as a means of connecting rehabilitation centres with. the highways. So, the urban development plans were connected to this. Accordingly, other urban parameters, schools, hospitals etc. were set up; expansion of education got a fillip too. Obviously, educated people of the landless section got a chance to fill these posts and led to intra-migration creating six towns within a decade.

After Tripura attained Statehood in 1972, there was a massive spurt of development leading to further urban growth (P.R. Bhattacharjee, 1993). The ground prepared by earlier plans yielded better agricultural productivity, irrigation and power infrastructure. Ambitious industrial programme was also endorsed - Jute mill, Sugar mill, Paper and Pulp mill (expenditure on industries shot up to about 7%) - which roped in landless/ migrant labours from the agricultural field. They started to inhabit the fringes of the urban units leading to further addition to the urban agglomeration, hence the number of town increased.

As is revealed from Table 1.1 during the span of 50 years 1901 to 1951 there was only one town which grew to six in the next decade as sub-divisional headquarters were built in the districts. It remained the same in 1971 too but increased to 10 in 1981 with two towns springing up in the South district and one each in West and North districts. In 1991 a total of 18 towns emerged in the State where West Tripura had the lion's share of 10 towns and four each in North and South. In 2001 the number of towns have increased to 23. The number of towns in west district has increased from 10 to 13. It may be noted here that another new district, namely Dhalai district, was created during the said period. In this newly created district another urban unit was declared town in 2001 census.

Table 1.1: Number of Towns in Tripura (1901-2001)

District	*1901-51*	*1961*	*1971*	*1981*	*1991*	*2001*
West Tripura	1	2	2	3	10	13
North Tripura	Nil	2	2	3	4	3
South Tripura	Nil	2	2	4	4	4
Dhalai	-	-	-	-	-	3
Tripura	1	6	6	10	18	23

Of the total population in 1901 which amounted to 1,73,325 only 6415 were urban i.e. meagre 3.70 per cent. The population rose to 2,29,613 in 1911 but urban growth was lesser this decade only 2.98 per cent i.e. 6831 in absolute numbers (Table 1.2). This downward trend continued for two more decades, 1921 and 1931. This was largely due to the fact that the population of Tripura was mainly agriculture dependent. Those who immigrated to the State were of similar profession and so decided to settle in the lush green valleys, lungas to practise wet rice cultivation urban centres did not lure them.

Table 1.2: Growth of Urban Population in Tripura (1901-2001)

Year	*Total*	*Urban*	*% of Urban Population*	*% of Decadal Growth*
1901	1,73,325	6,415	3.70	-
1911	2,29,613	6,831	2.98	6.48
1921	3,04,347	7,743	2.54	13.35
1931	3,82,450	9,580	2.50	23.72
1941	5,:13,010	17,693	3.45	84.69
1951	6,39,028	42,595	6.67	140.74
1961	11,42,05	1,02,997	9.02	141.81
1971	15,56,342	1,62,360	10.43	57.64
1981	20,53,058	2,25,568	10.99	38.93
1991	27,57,205	4,21,721	15.30	86.96
2001	31,91,168	5,43,094	17.02	28.78

In 1941 as population grew substantially, there was a growth in the urban population too amounting to 3.45 per cent. By 1941 communal atrocities, impending partition was forcing many to leave erstwhile East Pakistan for safer areas. Tripura, being the nearest State, with similar socio-economic scenario beckoned large numbers of immigrant. Pressure on land and land-related job increased to saturation point, by then even the tribal, the Manipuris were claiming their share of land for settled cultivation, hence a tendency of increased urban population was seen. The percentage increased from 3.45 to 6.67 in 1951 and further to 9.02 in 1961. The Bangladesh liberation war too acted as an impetus to population growth. By now people were flocking to the towns for urban jobs - white collared ones. The trend is since growing as can be seen in the decades of 1981, 1991 and 2001. However, it should be remembered that despite the growing urban population, the chunk of population is still agriculture-dependent. Uneconomic cultivation, disguised unemployment is rampant; but lack of infrastructure, lack of industrialisation all lead to concentration of people in the rural areas. Growth of population in urban centres of Tripura has been depicted in Table 1.3.. It appears from the table that Agartala (Population 189,327 - 2001 census) is only class-I category urban unit of the State.

Table 1.3: Growth of Population in Urban Centres of Tripura (1901-2001)

Census Year	*Cl.-VI below 5000*	*Cl.-V 5000 -9999*	*Cl.-IV 10,000 . 19,999*	*Cl.-III 20,000 . 49,999*	*Cl.-II 50,000. 99,999*	*Cl.-I 1,00,000 and above*	*Total Urban Population*
1901	-	6415	-	-	-	-	6415
1911	-	6831	-	-	-	-	6831
1921	-	7743	-	-	-	-	7743
1931	-	9580	-	-	-	-	9580
1941	-	-	17693	-	-	-	17693
1951	-	-	-	42595	-	-	42595
1961	-	34879	13240	-	54878	-	102997
1671	-	9338	52758	-	-	100264	162360
1681	7D28	13530	52018	20806	-	132186	225568
1991	9066	33384	105782	116131	-	157358	421721
2001	-	57842	114716	181209	-	189327	543094

REFERENCES

Bhattacharjee, P. R. (1993): *Economic Transition in Tripura,* Vikash Publishing, New Delhi.

Gibbs, Jack P. (1960) *Urban Research Methods,* Affiliated East - West.

Government of India, Census of India - Various Issues.

Government of Tripura, Directorate of Economics and Statistics, *Statistical Abstract,* Various Issues.

Khasnobis and Nath (1994): Urban growth and Urbanisation in West Bengal, Business Studies, C.U. Vol. XXII.

Krishnamurthy, J. (1984): Changes in the Indian workforce, *EPW,* Vol. XIX, No. 50.

Mitra, Ashok (1980): *Population and Area of Cities and Town and Urban Agglomerations,* 1872-1971, Allied, Calcutta.

Visaria, Pravin (1991): "India Population: Emerging perspective of the 1991 Census", *Demography - India,* Vol. 20 No. 2.

2

A Glimpse into the Structural Changes in Tripura

Each economic system has a complex internal structure and its performance can be assessed by the mutual relationship between its different component parts. Structural changes in an economy highlight the changing pattern of economic activities in various parts of the economy. The present section discusses the structural changes in the economy of Tripura.

State Domestic Product (SDP) is the sum total of goods and services produced by different sectors of a State during any particular year. The analysis of SDP data of Tripura highlights important structural changes during the period 1960-61 to 2002-03, such as increasing role of tertiary or secondary sector, etc. The shares of different sectors in the SDP of Tripura during the period 1960-61 to 2002-2003 are shown in Table 2.1. The data reveal that the contribution of the primary sector was 62.72 per cent in 1960-61, while the contributions of the secondary and tertiary sectors were only 5.71 per cent and 31.57 per cent respectively. The shares of the primary sector in SDP were highest during the period 1960-61 to 1980-81. However, share of the primary sector has declined gradually over the plan periods specially after 1980-81. In 1990-91 the share of the primary sector in SDP declined to 43.21 per cent. On the other hand, the contribution of the secondary sector reached to 25.57 per cent in 2000-2001 with variation over the years. But the interesting feature is that the contribution of tertiary sector has increased from 31.57 per cent in 1960-61 to 49.81 per cent in 1990-91. The contribution of tertiary sector has further increased to 54.91 per cent in 2002-2003. In 2000-01, the sector's contribution was 54.91 per cent. The contribution of secondary sector over this period has declined to 21.91 per cent in 2002-2003. And the contribution of primary sector has declined from 24.97 per cent in 2000-01 to 23.18 per cent in 2002-03. Thus it appears that the economy of the State dominated by primary sector continued till the eighties and after that tertiary sector continues to dominate the SDP. The contribution of secondary sector has increased significantly during nineties.

Table 2.1: Share of different Sectors in the State Domestic Product of Tripura (1961-61 to 2002-03)

(in percentage)

Sector	*1960-61*	*1970-71*	*1980-81*	*1990-91*	*2000-01*	*2002-03*
Primary Sector	62.72	70.02	60.22	43.21	24.97	23.18
Secondary Sector	05.71	07.01	08.55	06.98	25.57	21.91
Tertiary Sector	31.57	22.97	31.28	49.81	49.46	54.91
Total - (SDP)	100.00	100.00	100.00	100.00	100.00	100.00

Source:- Directorate of Economics & Statistics.

Note:- Share of all sectors in the above table have been expressed as a per cent of SDP at factor cost (at 1960-61 price for 1960-61 to 1980-81 and other at 1993-94 prices).

Share of different sectors in the SDP of Tripura by industry of origin during the period 1960-61 to 1999-2000 are shown in Table 2.2. From the table and the detailed data gathered from the Directorate of Economics and Statistics, it is revealed that in the primary sector, agriculture alone contributes nearly 85-95 per cent in primary sector of SDP. Others such as forestry and logging, fishing, mining and quarrying etc. contribute the rest. It is noteworthy to mention that the contribution of mining and quarrying has increased from Rs. 987 lakh in 1993-94 to Rs. 4779 lakh in 2000-01. The share of manufacturing has decreased from 5.71 per cent in 1960-61 to 0.94 per cent in 1999-2000.

Table 2.2: Share of different sectors in the State Domestic Product of Tripura by Industry of Origin (1960-61 to 2002-03)

(in percentage)

Sector	*1960-61*	*1970-71*	*1980-81*	*1990-91*	*2000-01*	*2002-03*
1. Agricultural & Allied.	62/72	70.02	60.22	43.21	24.37	23.18
2. Manufacturing	5.71	2.73	3.80	4.95	3.66	1.65
3. Construction Electricity, Gas, & Water Supply	-	4.28	4.70	2.05	21.91	20.26
4. Transport, Storage, Communication, Trade, Hotel & Restaurants, Finance, Banking, Insurance	17.51	13.36	15.20	16.88	22.55	25.86
5. Public Administration & Defence	7.61	4.07	8.94	14.78	13.35	14.53
6. Other service	6.45	5.54	7.14	18.40	13.56	14.51

Note : Share of all sectors have been expressed as a per cent of SDP at factor cost at 1960-61 prices for 1960-61 to 1980-81 and at 1993-94 prices for 2000 – 01 & 2002-03).

Source : Directorate of Economics & Statistics, Government of Tripura.

It implies that the decreased in the share of primary sector in SDP is not accompanied with increase in share of secondary sector rather it is tertiary sector which has increased substantially. According to available data the share of electricity, gas, water supply etc. was negative due to heavy losses in the public sector units. But the contribution of construction sector has increased significantly. Thus, the contribution of sector consisting of construction, electricity, gas, water supply etc.

has increased from 4.28 per cent in 1970-71 to 12.29 per cent in 1999-2000. The share of transport, storage, communication, trade, hotel, banking etc. has increased from 17.51 per cent in 1960-61 to 25.91 per cent in 1999-2000. This depicts a lopsided economy heavily dependent on service providing activities. The share of public administration has also increased remarkably from 7.61 per cent to 15.55 per cent during the period.

It is needless to mention that a corresponding change in the occupational classification of the work force is expected by these different sectors. Data on occupational classification of the population are not maintained and published annually. These are available only at decennial intervals through census data. Therefore the census data of 1951, 1961, 1971, 1981 and 1991 on occupational structure are considered for the analysis. However the occupational data of these censuses are not comparable in their original form, because the occupational categories and their definitions have undergone changes from one census to another. The 1951 census did not distinguish between working and non-working population. It classified livelihood category as agricultural and non-agricultural class. The 1961 census classified the population into two broad categories of workers and non-workers. The 1971 census concentrated only on the main activity of the person enumerated. Hence the census data left out a large number of workers, mostly the female population who were employed in agricultural work or some house-hold economic activity. This made the figure of workers not comparable with either the 1961 or the 1951 data. The census 1981 and 1991 distinguish between main workers, marginal worker, non-workers. Moreover these censuses classified the main workers into four simple categories. Thus these two census are comparable.

Independence and Tripura's integration with India witnessed far-reaching changes in the social, economic and political outlook of the State. Tripura became a Part C State in 1949, an Union Territory in 1956 and attained statehood in 1972. With this gradual transition of the princely State of Tripura to a modern constituent State of India, special efforts were made to put her economy in a proper order and also build up an infrastructure. In pre-Independence period, most of the workforce of the State depended upon agriculture and its allied activities. Though trade, industry, transportation was not exactly unheard of these were mainly carried out by residents of British India. Partition made Tripura a landlocked State, an enormous increase in transportation cost hindered industrial development and made her one of the most inaccessible frontier regions of India. The awarding of Chakla-Roshanabad (a fertile tract of 555 sq. miles) by the Radcliffe commission to erstwhile East Pakistan further limited Tripura's economic prospects because this plain land could contribute lavishly to the state's revenue as most of the peasants here carried out plough cultivation very successfully. Crippled by geographical isolation, with her population bursting at the seams, Tripura embarked upon an era of developmental progress since the Plan period of 1951.

Occupational pattern of the State has passed through several phases during the post independence era. A close look into the facts and figures may reveal certain manifestations of this pattern. The present paper is designed in this background. The object of this chapter is an in-depth analysis of the trend of occupational pattern of population in Tripura and occupational pattern of tribal population of the State.

The study is based on data collected from various issues of the Census Reports, Statistical Abstracts, Economic Reviews relating to the period of 1951-2001. The data on occupational classification of the population are not maintained and published annually but maintained at decadal intervals. However, the occupational data of these Censuses are not comparable in their original form as occupational categories and their definitions have undergone changes from one Census to another.

As is revealed in the 1951 Census data (Table 2.3) the population of the State was classified according to livelihood category into agricultural and non-agricultural class, no distinction was made between working and non-working population. As is seen, the agriculture class constituted of the major part of the population 4, 86, 881 persons or 75.4 per cent. Here it is also noteworthy that the owner-cultivators comprised of 3,84,147 persons or 59.5 per cent. This is mainly because after Independence there was a huge influx of immigrants from neighbouring erstwhile East Pakistan of which cultivators comprised the majority, also because there were no subsidiary occupation available able bodied men fell back upon agriculture as their only source of livelihood. At the same time the cultivating

Table 2.3: Livelihood Categories of Tripura's Population (1951 Census)

Livelihood Category	*Population*	*Per cent*
1. **Agriculture Class**	4,86,881	75.5
a) Cultivators of land wholly or mainly owned their dependents.	3,84,147	59.5
b) Cultivators of land wholly or mainly unowned and their dependents.	57,147	9.0
c) Cultivating labourers and their dependents.	31,886	4.9
d) Cultivating labourers of land, agricultural rent-receivers and their dependents.	12,918	2.0
2. **Non-Agriculture Class**	1,58,826	24.6
a) Production other then cultivation	38,395	5.9
b) Conveyance	40,838	6.4
c) Transport	3,314	0.5
d) Other Services and Misc.	76,279	11.8
Total Population	**6,45,707**	**100.0**

Source: Census Report, 1951.

labourers constituted only 4.9 per cent of the workers. This can be explained by the fact that as influx gathered momentum, land was initially reclaimed or 'created' to settle these new settlers, hence the small number of agricultural labourers at the initial years following Independence. However, those engaged in production other than cultivation were only 5.9 per cent of population. It may be stated here that even in the pre-Independence era as is seen in 1931 Census 7.8 per cent of the total workers were engaged in production. This shows a lack of industrial venture among the inhabitants of the State in the years following integration with India. Those engaged in other services, mainly administrative, education related jobs made a significant difference too as we find 11.8 per cent of the total population were engaged in these occupations.

Table 2.4: Total Workforce in Tripura (1951-2001)

	1951	*1961*	*1971*	*1981*	*1991*	*2001*
Main Worker	NA	NA	NA	6,08,589 (91.8)	7,93,457 (92.1)	9,12,292 (78.7)
Marginal Worker	NA	NA	NA	53,860 (8.13)	67,295 (7.82)	2,47,269 (21.32)
Total Workers	NA	7,37,229 (38.2)	4,32,463 (27.8)	6,62,449 (32.3)	8,60,752 (31.3)	11,59,561 (36.2)
Total Non-Workers	NA	7,04,776 (61.7)	11,23,879 (72.2)	13,90,609 (67.7)	18,84,075 (68.6)	20,39,642 (63.8)
Total Population	6,45,707	11,42,005	15,56,342	20,53,342	27,44,827	31,99,203

Source : Census Reports – Various Issues.

1. Percentages are shown within parentheses
2. Main Workers + marginal Workers = Total Workers
3. Total Workers + Total Non Workers = Total Population

As is evident from the Table 2.4 on workforce, the total workers of the State have increased noticeably in absolute numbers during the post-Independence period but their percentage share though initially 38.2 per cent has decreased, with 2001showing only 36.2 per cent of total population as workers. Similarly we find the non workers rise in numbers almost three fold. The workers were distinguished between marginal and main from the 1981 Census only. The marginal workers i.e. those who worked for less than 183 days in a year recorded a huge jump between 1981 and 2001-8.13 per cent to 21.32 per cent. To be more precise it was found that there were 67,295 marginal workers in 1991 which rose to 2,47,269 in 2001 and of these 95 per cent were residing in rural areas. It may be stated that as agricultural labourers too have increased enormously, these workers are the main contributing factor for increase in marginal workers during the said period.

The Census tables through the entire period of the present study make certain noteworthy revelations regarding the changing pattern of the occupational structure of the State. The Census of 1961 clearly distinguished between workers and non-workers. The change in occupational pattern in the last decade was almost non-existent though the percentage share of cultivators fell sharply (64.24 per cent), primary sector recorded a total of 74.56 per cent of the workforce. And this trend has continued throughout the period of study when we find that the cultivators share in the workforce, though have increased in absolute numbers their percentage share has actually fallen to 27 per cent in 2001. Simultaneously, the agricultural labourers have increased over the years at a much higher pace. In 1951 they were as low as 31,886 or 4.9 per cent only of the total population and they leapt up to 19.96 per cent in 1971, 22.05 per cent in 1981 though a slight fall was recorded in1991, 21.79 per cent, their percentage share increased to 23.81 per cent in 2001. Neither do we find any noticeable increase in the workforce engaged in household industries, rather their share fell from 5.75 per cent in 1961 to 3.04 per cent in 2001. Significantly though the increase in the numbers of those whose occupation is in the 'other services' is remarkable, from a modest 22.48 per cent in 1961 they doubled up to 46.12 per cent in 2001. (Table 2.5).

Table 2.5: Occupational Classification of Population in Tripura (1961-2001)

Classification of Workers	*1961*	*1971*	*1981*	*1991*	*2001*
Cultivators	2,80,881 (64.24)	2,35,292 (54.41)	2,63,427 (39.76)	3,05,523 (35.49)	3,13,300 (27.02)
Agricultural Labourers	32,912 (7.53)	86,340 (19.96)	1,46,089 (22.05)	1,87,538 (21.79)	2,76,132 (23.81)
Household industry workers	25,153 (5.75)	6,052 (1.39)	8,741 (1.82)	15,487 (1.79)	35,292 (3.04)
Others Labourers	98,283 (22.48)	1,04,779 (24.23)	2,44,192 (36.86)	3,52,204 (40.92)	5,34,837 (46.12)
Total Workers	4,37,229	4,32,463	6,62,449	8,60,752	11,59,561

Source: i) Census Reports – Various Issues
ii) *Statistical Abstract of Tripura* – Various Issues.

A quick scan of the data reveals that Tripura is still predominantly an agricultural State though the structure has varied to some extent. However, pressure of population on land has led to dwindling of the land holding which manifests itself in the growth of small and marginal holdings and reduction in the large holdings. This also accounts for the enormous growth of agricultural labourers due to rising trend of pauperisation along with land alienation among this section of the population. Though agriculture is losing its share in State income, the fast increase of essentially land dependent population without a corresponding increase in land availability or land related jobs obviously results in a surplus population engaged in agriculture. The consequence is underemployment which forces able bodied men to work as marginal workers and to become non-workers eventually.

As we know, the trend of developmental process is that primary occupation gradually makes way for secondary occupational structure. But as the occupational pattern reveals Tripura cannot wean her workforce from agriculture to the manufacturing sector because of absence of any industrial base. The over crowded agricultural sector is also characterized by absence of adequate modern techniques, inadequate irrigation facilities, failure to switch over to intensive cultivation etc. And these cannot be explained in terms of ignorance alone. Unfavorable industrial climate, predominance of unorganized sector, traditional and village based industries inhibits the absorption of the workers into the secondary sector. Hence our planners, realizing the limitations started to put the hilltops into productive use. Horticulture, plantations, animal husbandry and later planned forestry were gradually introduced. An additional advantage of this was that the tribesmen could easily be roped into these land-based agricultural activities thus "shifting" them away from uneconomic jhuming. Tea plantation in Tripura, though has a long history did not record any booster growth over the years, however, those employed here has increased by over 38 per cent during 1957-88. Plantation crops like rubber, cashew nut, areca-nut are playing a very important role in the state's economy since the 1960s. Moreover, rubber has an excellent opportunity for expanding Tripura's agro-industrial base to provide employment to the state's rural population. Other activities of the primary sector, i.e. animal husbandry, pisciulture, livestock rearing etc. have gained a stronghold in today's economy. But the huge army of agricultural labourers, marginal workers and non workers show that these avenues perhaps are yet to be exploited to its full extent. Lack of adequate knowledge, inadequate finances, attitude etc. inhibits the extensive spread of these allied jobs.

Table 2.5 also reveals the growth of the "Other labourers" sector, from a modest number of 98,283 or 22.48 per cent in 1961to whopping number of 5,34,837 or 46.12 per cent of the total workforce. Undoubtedly, urbanization has made rapid strides in Tripura since Independence. Though slow initially during 1991-2001 urban growth has been recorded to be 34.38 per cent against a similar growth of urban population of 31.13 per cent at the all India level. Present urban population of Tripura stands to be 17.02 per cent. Hence an overall orientation of the region in terms of trade, commerce, services, transportation, education has taken place and urbanisation has been an added incentive for the people to take up white collared jobs. The increases in educational opportunities in Tripura have evoked adequate response from all communities and have provided employment to a large number of people in office work.

The decline in the percentage share of cultivators and the corresponding rise in agricultural labour points to a basic change in the occupation pattern of the tribal society. With the rising pressure of population on land the self subsistent economy of the hills men was giving way to one of a wider kind. The tribesmen faced a dilemma – whether to seek refuge in remoter hills or change over to settled cultivation during the decade following Independence. The elite among them, the chieftains did change over, they came into contact with the new settlers, learnt the amenities of a money economy, the advantages of a social life and soon got into the habit of borrowing even. A new evil penetrated into thei closed society that of indebtedness. Owing to hand-to-mouth conditions, with consumption loans accumulating over time, the hills men had to virtually hypothecate their crops and ultimately land even. Plantations, jhumiya rehabilitation schemes, credit facilities, even spread of education among brought them in contact with urban life. But absence of manufacturing units, their unskilled nature force them to work as daily labourers, often underpaid. Hence the small numbers of tribal workers in trade, commerce, construction work etc. The rural tribesmen obviously prefers land related occupations but certain policies which had to be implemented to accommodate the migrants created much animosity in the mind of the users of land. As we find the huge increase of agricultural labourers among the tribes occurred in

1971-81 this was an important factor in the outbreak of violent outbursts during the 1980s and militancy in the 1990s. One should remember that a large section of the tribesmen of our State depended upon 'shifting cultivation' but as land available dwindled, they had difficulty to accustom themselves to the new socio-economic set up. Some moved to the remoter hills, hence were cut off from mainstream developmental progress.

The latest occupational classification of workforce perhaps substantiates for the foregoing analysis of the changing occupational pattern of the workforce of Tripura. As we can notice cultivators are the least in Tripura as compared to all the States of the North East, similarly agricultural labour is the highest (Table 2.6). Those working in the household industries are somewhat higher than a few States with manufacturing units gaining momentum. But again those involved in the 'other services' shows a huge increase in Tripura's case.

Table 2.6: Occupational Classification of Workforce in North-East States (2001 Census)

Name of the States	*Total Workers*	*Cultivators*	*Agricultural Labour*	*House*	*Other*
Assam	100	39.1	13.2	3.6	44.0
Arunachal Pradesh	100	57.8	3.9	1.3	37.0
Manipur	100	40.2	12.0	10.3	37.6
Meghalaya	100	48.1	17.7	2.2	32.0
Mizoram	100	54.9	05.7	1.5	37.9
Nagaland	100	64.7	3.6	2.6	29.0
Sikkim	100	49.9	6.5	1.6	42.0
Tripura	100	27.0	23.8	3.0	46.1
India	**100**	**32.9**	**38.9**	**6.5**	**21.7**

Source: Census Report, 2001.

Concluding Remarks

An analysis of the structure of occupations have revealed that certain changes have undoubtedly occurred not a drastic transformation. Though investments in secondary sector has increased since Independence this have not been able to shift the workforce from primary activities. Various incentives provided by the Government have not been able to attract enterprises even. This shows that even in the threshold of a new century Tripura has a long way to go before embarking upon the path of economic progress. There is an urgent requirement for a change in the occupational pattern so that a large section of the workers can be accommodated in industrial and services sector thus relieving the pressure on agriculture. This will also lead to an increase in agricultural productivity as mechanization, consolidation of holding, use of better quality seeds fertilisers etc. will grow hand-in-hand in diversifying Tripura's primary sector Gradual growth of secondary sector brought forth by technical or vocational education, entrepreneurship training programmes, will also lead to a change in the youth's attitude, preferences, values etc. This will divert them from their fascination of white collared jobs and make them seek a way out through self employment setting up innovative enterprises. We should remember that the growth of services sector alone cannot solve the problems of the State. A change in the pattern of occupations will also lead to better communication facility, set aside transport bottlenecks, open up trade and commerce – thus embarking upon new vistas of employment. As the last two sectors expand the three activities may be linked together thus ushering in a welcome change in the occupational structure.

A brief analysis of the tables reveal that though Tripura is primarily an agricultural State, the occupational structure has become varied with too much pressure on land. Cultivation is the mainstay still but land has other utilisation too in this tiny border State with the population bursting at the seams. It is but quite natural an economic process that as cultivators decline, agricultural labourers shoot up, that is what is happening here too. If there were industries, such uneconomic labour force could be engaged but with a weak infrastructure that probability is ruled out. Trade and commerce, transport could be another occupation which would absorb a sizeable population of this category but being a border State, almost landlocked, except for that narrow strip through Assam, this trade does not get due importance. Thus may be explained the huge and rising number of non-workers through the decades.

It is noted earlier that the contribution of primary sector in SDP of Tripura has declined to a noticeable extent and the contribution of tertiary sector has increased on the other hand. But in spite of a continuous decline in contribution of primary sector, the occupational structure has not changed to that extent. Thus the main feature of the structural change is the failure of the occupational structure to coincide with the sectoral changes in SDP. The maximum portion of the working people still depend on the primary activities for their livelihood. In 1961 about 74.56 per cent of the work-force were engaged in the primary sector consisting of agriculture, forestry, fishery etc. Although this figure declined to 64.08 per cent in 1991, this sector still houses the largest portion of the work force in the State. While the primary sector contributed 62.72 per cent of SDP in 1960-61 and only 43.21 per cent in 1990-91. So it can be concluded that although a greater portion of the work force in the State engaged in primary sector, its contribution to SDP has declined significantly and does not coincide with each other. The aspect of structural change showing a substantial decline of primary sector in SDP, no doubt, is the sign of development. But the other aspect showing decline of work force in primary sector has not been to the expected proportion. This is because of failure of other sectors to absorb not only the growing number of workforce from new entrants but also to divert a substantial portion of workforce from primary sectors. Another significant feature within the occupational pattern in primary sector is that increasing number of agricultural labourers in the State. It was 7.53 per cent in 1961 and increased to 23.38 per cent in 1991. This implies the growing problem of landlessness of the rural people of Tripura, (Bhattacharjee, P.R. 1993,p.86).

As regards structural change in the distribution of SDP between commodity and non-commodity, it is observed that the non-commodity has been growing much than the commodity sector. The changing share of the modern sector in SDP is also one of the indicators of structural change in the State economy. This can be perceived by the increasing role of trade, transport, communication, etc. in the SDP. The share of transport, storage, communication, hotel, trade etc. has increased from 17.51 per cent in 1960-61 to 25.91 per cent in 1999-2000.

It is observed that the tertiary sector in Tripura has developed before the matured development in the secondary sector. With the expansion of transport, trade and commerce, the contribution of the tertiary sector has also been increasing in the State. However, increase in this sector may not be taken as an indicator of growth in terms of real output of the State.

REFERENCES

Agarwal, A.K. (1988) : *North Eastern Economy : Problems and Prospects,* Mittal Publications, New Delhi.

Bhattacharjee, P.R. (1993) : *Economic Transition in Tripura,* Vikash Publishing, New Delhi.

Chakraborty, D. (2004) : *Land Question in Tripura,* Akansha Publishing House, New Delhi.

Chakraborty, K.S. (2005) : 'Structural Change and Strategy of Development Resource – Industry linkage in Tripura', in *Structural Change and Strategy of Development,* ed. by Gurudas Das, Akansha Publishing House, New Delhi.

Government of India, Census Reports, Various Issues.

Government of Tripura, Directorate of Economics and Statistics: Statistical Abstract, various Issue.

Land Acquisition Department – No. 2509 – 10/DM/LA/SS/60/54 dt. 4th March, 1957. (Tripura Secretariat Archives)

North Eastern Council: *Basic Statistics of North Eastern Region,* 2002, Shillong.

3

State Plan Expenditure in Tripura: An Overview

To achieve any target within a given time period we have to go for planning to arrange all the resources, parameters in a rational way. Planning, we know, is an instrument of economic development. This chapter critically discusses the expenditure in State plan of Tripura.

In Tripura, development planning started in 1951, beginning of a new era in economic development process. The economic set up of the State was somewhat dislocated, so infrastructure was to be built up, roads and communications, medical facilities, agriculture to be modernised, rehabilitation of the displaced people, education and welfare of the weaker sections.

Table 3.1 reveals an outstanding fact at the very first glance, there is a giant leap forward between the First and the Second Five-year Plan so far as planned investment is concerned. Tripura had not attained Statehood in the First Five-year Plan period hence the total plan outlay was Rs 197.86 (crore) with transport and communication getting the maximum benefit – 37.40 per cent followed by social and community welfare – 34.16 per cent, cooperation got only 14.30 per cent while agriculture still needed much modernisation as only 8.46 per cent was allotted for this. Second Five-year Plan (1956-61) allotted Rs.896.10(crore) of which infrastructure building took up quite a sizeable amount, road network was completed by the Second Five-year Plan period hence further investment needed for transport and communication (40.45). As can be seen from the table, social and community services also received priority

Table 3.1: Sector-wise plan expenditure in Tripura

(First to Sixth Five-year Plans)

Name of the Sector	*First Plan (1951-56)*	*Second Plan (1956-61)*	*Third Plan (1961-66)*	*FourthPlan (1969-74)*	*Fifth Plan (1974-78)*	*Sixth Plan (1980-85)*
1. Agriculture & Allied Service	8.46	14.51	22.45	18.19	24.12	24.89
2. Co-operation	14.30	1.78	1.86	1.38	1.59	1.98
3. Irrigation and power	2.70	3.76	4.23	28.86	30.45	24.68
4. Industries & Minerals	2.98	4.76	4.62	1.83	6.99	4.12
5. Transport & Communications	37.40	40.45	27.52	24.43	14.18	12.73
6. Social Community	34.16	34.70	37.94	24.74	22.32	30.31
7. Economic Service	-	0.04	1.13	0.07	0.17	0.15
8. General Service	-	-	0.24	0.50	0.18	1.14
	100 (197.86)	100 (896.10)	100 (1597.49)	100 (3541.13)	100 (4967.42)	100 (29271.41)

Source : Directorate of Economics & Statistics, Government of Tripura

during the entire Plan Period hovering around 34-35 per cent. Due emphasis was given to refugee rehabilitation programme, tribal welfare, jhumia settlements. Education and medical services also required much. However, agriculture, power and irrigation were not among top priorities during the First and Second Five-year Plans. Tribal economy basically was *jhum*-based which had already started posing ecological problems as well as low productivity and sustaining capacity. Wet-rice cultivation was just gaining grounds without the advent of the immigrants from East Pakistan, there was ample scope for increasing agricultural production.

The Third Plan also showed similar variations, except for the fact that spending on transport and communication was lowered (27.52per cent) perhaps because the road network work was completed by the end of Second Plan period. Agriculture received a spurt this time, the allotted sum was 22.45 per cent of the total outlay. Social service (37.97 per cent) too increased while economic (1.13) and general services (0.24) were gaining a foothold in sum allocation. However, power and irrigation, industries and mineral still lagged behind 4.23 per cent and 4.62 per cent respectively. After the Third Plan, the Fourth Five-year Plan could not be started. Thus three annual plans were formulated by the Government of India-1966-67, 1967-68, 1968-69 aiming at bridging the gap in the planning process. In Tripura's case it was found that a huge amount of outlay was made in the Fourth Plan (1969-74) i.e. Rs 35.41 crores and this further increased manifold henceforth. .In the Fourth Plan, a rise in the allotment was seen in the power and irrigation sector (28.86 per cent) at least a six times increase since the Third Plan. Agriculture allotment was reduced (18.19 per cent) while the same happened in transport and communication though marginally.

During the Fifth Plan the most outstanding fact was that more than 30 per cent of plan expenditure was made on power and irrigation. It should also be mentioned that agriculture too received 24.12 per cent of the total expenditure as well as industries and minerals received 6.99 per cent. A jute mill, a sugar mill, paper and pulp mill were set up, this is an achievement undoubtedly as only 1.83 per cent was laid aside during the last plan. Transport and communication could not boast of huge fund allocation (14.18 per cent) as all essential construction of roads, bridges were completed except for railways and tele-communications. Social and community services still received high priority in the matter of fund allocation (22.34 per cent).

Once again two year of Rolling plan (1978-80) had to be initiated. The allocation pattern of Plan fund during the Sixth Plan period showed another giant leap in terms of total outlay, Rs 292.71 crores. Expenditure went up enormously, but the allocation procedure almost resembled the Fifth Plan.

In the Seventh Plan (1985-90) there was a total restructuring of the heads of development. Economic services meant agriculture and allied services, rural development, special programmes, industry etc., as shown Table 3.2. Under social services were categorised education, sports, medical, welfare etc. Rest came under general services. Agriculture got the top priority in the Seventh Plan 16.35 per cent followed by energy, 11.63 per cent while transport received 11.08 per cent. Irrigation and flood control received 8.37 per cent while social service still maintained a high of 31.34 per cent. The heads, which got due importance during the seventh plan, was rural development sector (7.16 per cent) and Special Area Programme (7.45 per cent). These catered to the Tripura Tribal Areas Autonomous District Council linked to tribal areas development. It is also remarkable that opening of schools, medical facilities received priority during this plan period as well as provision of basic civic amenities (housing, water supply) so necessary for the growing urbanisation. The Eighth plan once again showed similar characteristics of plan expenditure. The heads, which were stressed upon, were similar to the last plan. However, transport sector dwindled in its fund allocation structure from 11.08 to 9.29 per cent. A new need was added perhaps to cope up with environmental pollution that is forestry and wild life where 2.30 per cent of plan expenditure was allocated. The Ninth Plan, however, shows varied changes, agriculture allotment reduced of below half 6.53 per cent, while rural development gained immensely - 13.84 per cent. Irrigation and flood control received higher allocation - 7.53 while transport once again received more funds, 14.25 per cent. Significantly, expenditure allocated for Energy purpose dwindled to 6.80 per cent and even industry and mineral allocation (3.08 per cent) social service continued to get higher allocation – 40 per cent of the total outlay, forestry fund was almost helved 1.06 per cent.

The analysis of plan expenditure gives both qualitative and quantitative aspects during plan period. Obviously Tripura witnessed a spurt in the economic activities of the government stressing upon infrastructure requirement. Quite a lump sum was later allocated for development and modernisation of agriculture as also industrial base, it is another story that this dream could not be realised owing to other reasons. Throughout the period the Government's concern with social and community services (education, medical facilities, welfare of the weaker service etc.) was predominant.

So far as the growth of SDP is concerned it has risen from Rs 28.38 lakh in 1960-61 to Rs.86.82 lakh in 1987-88 at constant price (1960-61). The per capita income during the same period has also increased from Rs 248.53 lakh to Rs. 321.56 lakh. At constant price of 1980-81 the SDP has grown from Rs 26261 lakh in 1980-81 to Rs 48969 lakhs in 1992-93.The per capita income during this period has also increased from Rs. 1297 to Rs. 1913 lakh. Excessive population growth owing to mass scale immigration in the State is one of the main reasons for low rate of growth in per capita income. However the SDP at constant price (1993-94) has increased from Rs. 161927 lakh in 1993-94 to Rs. 246531 lakh in 1999-2000 and Rs. 260739 in 2000-01 (quick estimate). On the other hand per capita income during this period has increased from Rs. 5350 to Rs.6604 and Rs. 6813 respectively.

To accelerate the development of the scheduled tribes in Tripura, a special strategy was adopted from the Fifth 5 year Plan. This is known as 'Tribal Sub-Plan' (TSP). The TSP strategy is a mechanism under which each development departments of the State Government is required to qualify and set aside an amount of their plan budget provision for implementation of schemes exclusively for the welfare of schedule tribes. Such fund should not be less than the percentage of schedule tribe population in the State. According to an estimate an amount of Rs. 14716.71 lakhs was spent on TSP in the year 2000-01.

Table 3.2: Sector-wise Plan Expenditure in Tripura

(Seventh to Tenth Plan)

(in percentage of total expenditure)

Name of Sector		Seventh plan	Eighth plan	Ninth plan	Tenth Plan
A.	*Economic Service –*				
1.	Agriculture and Allied Activities	16.35	18.00	6.53	10.00
2.	Rural Development	7.16	6.52	13.84	12.00
3.	Special area programme	7.45	8.00	5.44	7.00
4.	Irrigation and Flood Control	8.37	6.63	7.53	8.00
5.	Energy	11.63	10.73	6.80	5.00
6.	Industry and Mineral	4.63	5.72	3.08	3.00
7.	Transport	11.08	9.29	14.25	16.83
8.	Communication	0.00	0.00	0.04	0.20
9.	Science, Tech. and Env.	0.46	0.31	0.12	0.30
10.	Gen. Economic Service	0.43	0.63	0.47	1.50
B.	*Social Service*	31.34	30.97	40.00	40.50
C.	*General Service.*	1.36	0.87	0.93	1.50
D.	*Forestry and Wild life.*	-	2.30	1.06	00.00
		100	100	100	100

Source : Directorate of Economics and Statistics, Government of Tripura

Similarly the Special Component Plan (SCP) strategy for the welfare of schedule castes was introduced during the Sixth Plan period. It is a mechanism under which various State Government departments are required to quantify and set aside on amount of their own plan budget provision for various welfare activities of the scheduled caste population in the State. The quantified amount should not be less than the percentage of schedule caste population in the State. To implement the programme under SCP, the State Government has identified 298 gram panchayet villages having SC concentration. The SCP outlay for the year 2000-01 was Rs. 66.10 crores as against a total State plan outlay of Rs. 4815 cores. This is 13.62 per cent of the total State plan outlay and 20.69 per cent of the divisible State plan outlay.

4

Marketing Channel of Agricultural Produces in Tripura

In earlier days when the village economy was more or less self-sufficient the marketing of agricultural produce did not face any difficulty as the farmers sold their produce to the consumers on a cash or barter basis. In modern days marketing of agricultural produce has to undergo a series of transfers or exchanges from one hand to another before it finally reaches the consumer. This is achieved through three marketing functions (a) assembling, (b) preparation for consumption and (c) distribution. Concentration pertains to the operations concerned with the assembly and transport from the field to a common assembly field or market. The produce may be taken direct to the market or it may be stored on the farm or in the village for varying periods before its transport. It may be sold as obtained from the field or may be cleaned, graded, processed and packed either by the farmer or village merchant before it is taken to the market. Some of the processing is done not because consumers desire it, but because it is necessary for the conservation of quality. At the market the farmer may sell the produce directly to the consumer or more usually through a commission agent or a broker. Traders, wholesalers or retailers may also purchase it. The transactions may be carried out by direct negotiation or through middlemen, by barter or cash, by open or under cover auction, on the spot or in future markets. The transactions take place at one or more levels in the primary, secondary or terminal markets or all three. Distribution (dispersion) involves the operations of wholesaling and retailing at various points. By a series of indispensable adjustments and equalising functions, it is the task of the distribution system to match the available supplies with the existing demand.

The transfer of produce or goods takes place through a chain of middlemen or agencies. In the primary market the main functionaries are the producer, the village or itinerary merchant, pre-harvest contractors, commission agents, transport agents etc. In the secondary market the processing and manufacturing agents are the additional functionaries. Financing agents such as shroffs, banks and co-operatives may also take part. In the terminal or export market the commercial analyst and shipping agent also gets involved in the transfer of goods.

The functionaries have their own set up. They may be individuals, partners or co-operatives who may buy and sell on ready and future basis at a price determined by forces of supply and demand. Each functionary renders some service in the process of marketing and also earns a varying margin of profit for himself. This procedure makes marketing rather complicated and inflates the price of the produce. The nature of some of the agricultural products for their bulk form and perishability and their seasonal availability further add to the complexity of agricultural marketing.

Economic development has come to be associated with industrialisation. It is however, considered that industrilisation can follow only on the sound heels of agriculture. Hence, agricultural progress is regarded as prerequisite of economic development. In the process of development, agriculture has to be given priority in order to accelerate the rate of economic progress. In Tripura, the vital role of agriculture arises out of the position the agrarian sector occupies in the overall economy of the state. The primary sector, as has already been pointed out is the largest sector of economic activity and it has a crucial role to play in the state's economic development by providing food grain and raw materials, employment to a large population and also forming capital. The State's agrarian sector is basically in the form of rudimentary nature of cultivation. In such situation there is no scope for any disagreement that growth of agricultural production is necessary for its survival. The present chapter deals in identifying the marketing channels of agricultural produces of Tripura on the basis of the survey conducted in this connection.

Marketing of agricultural produces include all the business activities involved in moving produces from widely scattered produces to the ultimate customers. In the process the agricultural produces undergo a change in time, place, ownership and sometimes even in form which adds to their value. The chains of intermediaries through which the various produces pass between farmers and consumers constitute their marketing channels.

The marketing channels for all the vegetables, food grains, other then paddy-rice, cotton, jute, pan etc. are different in Tripura. The channels of distribution of paddyrice, vegetable and fruits as identified in the agricultural marketing in Tripura, are discussed below.

The agricultural produces that are marked in the rural markets of Tripura come mainly from two sectors, the cultivators operating the smallholdings and those tilling relatively large sized holdings. Most of the transactions in rural markets involve small quantities of agricultural produces. Marketing channels for paddy-rice, vegetables and fruits in Tripura are discussed below.

Five market channels for paddy-rice have been identified in the sample markets. They are:

(i) Cultivator-Consumer or Direct Sale,

(ii) Cultivator-Miller cum Trader-Consumer,

(iii) Cultivator-Miller-Wholesaler-Retailer-Consumer,

(iv) Cultivator-Trader-Miller cum Wholesaler-Consumer,

(v) Cultivator-Paikar-Terminal Wholesaler-Miller-Retailer-Consumer.

It is observed in the rural markets of Tripura that paddy-rice in small quantities processed with indigenous technology occupies the major share of transactions through the channel of direct sale. It is also observed that purchase of commodities and payments of any dues in exchange of paddy-rice are very common in the rural markets of Tripura. This type of transactions may also be included in the channel of direct sale. Besides direct sale, the channel, cultivators-miller-cum-trader-consumer is one of the important marketing channel found in the sample markets of Tripura. It is seen in the sample markets that the millers with selling outlets in the nearby markets frequently buy paddy, mill it and sell to the consumer with a good margin. Infact, rice millers play a dominant role in the marketing of paddy-rice and Tripura is no exception. The presence of rice millers and their active involvement in the marketing process are found in almost all the sample markets. They not only, process or sell the paddy but sometimes even store it for future price rise.

Among the other indentified channel of marketing, the channel, cultivator-paikar-terminal wholesaler-miller-retailer-consumer, is perhaps the most common effective marketing channel, having much commercial relevance in the state. Existence of paikar during the paddy-marketing season has become a common feature of every rural market. These paikars usually are outsiders. They come to the respective village during the season and stay in a rented house near the markets. They prefer to buy or collect paddy instead of rice and and finally send the same to wholesalers at Agartala (terminal market), and finally rice reaches the customer through the retailers.

Turning to the vegetable marketing, three market channels are identified in the sample markets. These are:

(i) Farmer-Consumer or Direct Sale,

(ii) Farmer-local arhyatdar-trader-consumer,

(iii) Farmer-paikar-retailer-consumer.

It is found in the rural markets of Tripura that higher priced produces and small quantity items are sold through direct sale. Sizeable portions of vegetables, are, however, marketed through the channel of farmer-local arhyatdar-trader-consumer. Arhyatdar collects the produce from the farmers and sell to the vegetable traders of nearby markets. They even supply to the retailers of the sub-divisional towns of Tripura. The farmers who produce large quantity on commercial basis sell their vegetable produces to the paikars of the terminal markets and use the third channel i.e. farmer –paikar-retailer-consumers. On market days, many agents of paikar or wholesalers come to these markets and collect the produces, transport these immediately to terminal markets.

In case of fruits marketing, the following marketing channels are found in Tripura.

i) Farmer – Consumer or Direct Sale.

ii) Farmer – Local Agent –trader-consumer

iii) Farmer – Local Agent –wholesalers –Traders – Consumers

iv) Farmer - Local Agent –wholesalers –paikar -Traders – Consumers

As the fruits are perishable and are not commercially produced in Tripura except pineapple, these products follow the above-mentioned channels of distribution, which are different in terms of nature of transactions from other agricultural produces. It is observed in the rural markets that the marketing channels of fruits through direct sale i.e. farmer-consumer are insignificant in the process of marketing. In most of the sample markets this channels of distribution is found absent. A large numbers of middlemen are found involved in the process of marketing of fruits. The channel farmers-local agent-wholesalers–paikars–traders-consumer is found operative and a more effective channel. The presence of local collecting agent and paikars at the terminal distribution level are the distinct features of identification marketing channels of fruits.

In the marketing of agricultural process the farmers have been in all cases a price taker. Therefore, if the farmer's share in the consumer's price is inadequate he will not be encouraged for further production. The presence of large number of middlemen in transactions of agricultural produces through the identified channels are found in the suvey of sample markets. Direct sale. i.e. without involving middlemen are also seen during the study but the number of such transactions are quite poor in comparison to total transactions. Therefore, the development of direct marketing of agricultural produces is discussed below.

There are many channels involved in marketing of agricultural produces. The following are the factors for the selection of efficient marketing channels.

1. Reasonable return to producer.
2. Transportation cost in that channel.
3. Commission charges and market margins received by the intermediaries.
4. Financial resources.
5. Shorter channel with minimum market cost.

In agricultural marketing 'Direct Marketing' is perhaps the only channel suitable for both the consumers and cultivators. In Tripura it is a long felt need of the farmers and consumers as it goes a long way in ensuring higher remuneration to the farmers and meeting the satisfaction level of the consumers through direct sale of the agricultural commodity by the farmers to the consumer at affordable prices. Direct marketing of agricultural produce helps to eliminate middle men and commission agents who charge high level of commission fee from the farmers coming to the markets for selling their produce and then artificially inflate the retail prices. The efficacy of direct agricultural marketing infrastructure facility can be increased by providing market user common facilities for proper weighing, cleaning, grading and packaging of agricultural produce being brought to the market yard by the farmers for sale. In order to give a big boost to the development of direct agricultural marketing infrastructure facilities in the country, the Government of India, Ministry of Agriculture has announced the "Scheme for Development/ Strengthening of Agricultural Marketing Infrastructure, Grading and Standardisation." Under the scheme credit linked back ended subsidy to the tune of 25% of the total project cost (33.33% of the total project cost for projects in North East states), is available. Development of direct marketing infrastructure forms one of the components of the scheme.

It is observed that regulated market yards for fruits and vegetables are functioning only at a few centres in Tripura. It is found that the marketing system for fruits and vegetables is now in the hands of middlemen. Middlemen exist at various levels between the farmers and the consumers and exploit through malpractice in weighment, handling and payments. Large numbers of small farmers are unable to effectively bargain for better price in the wholesale market. Inefficiencies in the wholesale markets results in a long chain of intermediaries, multiple handling, loss of quality and increase the gap between the producer and consumer prices. Large numbers of small retailers, each handling small quantities, create high overheads leading to high margin on produces.

It is therefore felt necessary to evolve an alternate marketing strategy where both growers and consumers are benefited through this kind of market. Cultivators' market was introduced with a view to eliminate the middlemen and arrange facilities for the farmers to sell their produce directly to the consumers at reasonable rates fixed every day. On account of the scheme both the farmers and the consumers are benefited.

Cultivators' market is thus planned for direct interface between the farmers and the consumers eliminating middlemen. Cultivators' Market, if function effectively, can act as price stabilization centers. The development of cultivators' Market in Tripura is necessary for the following purposes.

a) To ensure remunerative prices to the rural farmers and provide fresh vegetables to the consumers at reasonable rates fixed every day.

b) To provide direct interface between farmers and consumers- eliminating intermediaries in trade.

c) To facilitate prompt realization of sale proceeds to the farmers without any deductions.

d) To curb malpractice in weighment.

Successful operation of direct agricultural marketing depend upon location of the bazars, number of customers visiting the bazar per day, nature, type, quantity and quality of agricultural produce being brought by the farmers for sale, systematization of the retail price fixation mechanism, allotment of stalls to the farmers on farmers' group basis, design of the stalls based on the nature, type and quantity of salable items brought by the farmers, availability of functional infrastructure facilities viz. cleaning, grading, weighing, packaging, short term storage etc., price display mechanism, broadcasting system, availability of utilities viz. electricity, water, garbage disposal/ cleaning facilities and last but not the least service facilities for the convenience of the consumers viz. parking, banks with coin changing machines, grievance redress mechanism etc. The facilities should, therefore, match to the requirement of the farmers and the consumers.

NABARD is the apex financial institution of the country for agriculture and rural development and plays a vital role in coordinating all financial banks, state agencies etc. to develop the countryside. As a pro-active role, it formulates broad strategies and fixes technical specifications, disseminates information and extends financial assistance to the agencies for development of agricultural marketing infrastructure facilities to tap the potential and protect the interest of the rural community in general and farming community in particular. As direct agricultural marketing infrastructure facilities like Farmers' Markets play an important role in the economic developmental process of the farming community, this bulletin is prepared as a reference document for bankers, farmers and other developmental agencies. NABARD provides refinance and co-finanace support to various eligible financing banks for financing development of direct agricultural marketing infrastructure under its normal refinance programme. This bulletin can be utilised in identifying the potential Farmers' Markets and formulating schemes for the development of the infrastructure with NABARD refinance support. The Department of agriculture (Marketing), Government of Tripura may take the advantage of the above schemes.

5

Marketing Costs and Margins in Transactions of Agricultural Produces in Tripura

The present chapter is an attempt to assess the marketing costs and margins of agriculture produces in Tripura. The average marketing costs and margins of marketing agencies in consumer price of rice, vegetables and fruits, available and transported from selected regulated markets to terminal market are analysed in this chapter. The variation of cultivators share, if any, among the farmers in tribal dominated markets and non-tribal dominated markets are also discussed. The study is based on the extensive survey made in a few selected regulated markets of Tripura. Out of 21 regulated markets in the State, five markets namely Bishalgarh, Sonamura, Garjee, Nutan Bazar and Kulai are considered as sample regulated markets to assess the marketing costs and margins. Of these, three regulated markets namely Garjee, Nutan Bazar and Kulai are tribal dominated markets while Bishalgarh and Sonamura are non-tribal dominated markets. The movement of agricultural produces from the above-mentioned markets to the state's only terminal market, Agartala, occupies a sizeable share in the total transactions of terminal market. The study deals with certain number of transactions during the year 2002. In dealing with the issues the study relies upon the information gathered on the basis of discussions made with cultivators, cultivator-cum-traders, consumers, middleman, arhyatdars, dealers, transport operators and other persons involved in the marketing process of sample markets. Price of agricultural produces at sub-divisional level and at terminal market level have also been cross checked to arrive at consumer price.

Meaning and Significance

Marketing costs are the actual expenses incurred in the marketing process. They include not only the cost of performing the various marketing functions but different levies as well. The costs of performing the marketing function include transportation cost, labour charges, packaging, storing, processing etc. Marketing margins are actual amounts received by the marketing agencies in the marketing process.

The marketing margins between the cultivator and the consumer may be taken as index of the soundness of the marketing set up of any produce. A number of studies stand to confirm that a large number of middlemen function at various stages of agricultural marketing in India and they reduce the share of the consumer's price. The prices spread in Indian market is thus considerable and the cultivator's share of the consumer's rupees is very small. Retailers and wholesalers together often grab as much as 40 paise out of every rupees paid by the consumer. This highlights the high marketing cost and relatively high marketing costs indicate the inefficient market pattern.

Tripura has, in fact, two types of cultivation in the two distinct topographical regions. Nearly one-third of the population, the tribesmen, mainly dwell in the hills and sustain living by a primitive method of cultivation known locally as "Jhum". The rest of the population live on the plains and practice settled cultivation with semi-modern or modern techniques. The market arrivals of agricultural produce in Tripura may broadly be grouped as food grains, vegetables and fruits. Rice constitutes the major share in food grains. Vegetables include the various kinds of vegetables consumed and fruits include locally available fruits like banana, jackfruit, pineapple, wood apple, lichi, etc. The market shares of other agriculture produces are negligible and their market arrivals are also irregular.

So far as market scenario is concerned, there are at present, altogether 564 markets in the state, of which 474 are primary markets and 83 are wholesale assembling markets and 7 municipal markets. The state has 21 regulated markets and only one terminal market situated at the state capital, Agartala.

Findings and Discussions

The marketing costs and margins involved in transactions of agricultural produces i.e. rice, vegetables and fruits, in sample markets are presented in Tables 5.1.and 5.2.

It is evident from Table 5.1 that cultivator's average share in consumer's price in the sample markets varies between 65.82 to 72.06 per cent in case of rice marketing. While the Miller's and Wholesaler's margin varies between 6.15 and 9.53 per cent in consumer's price. And retailer's average margin are between 9.80 to 14.82 per cent. Therefore, it can be said that the retailers and wholesalers consume as much as 15.95 to 24.35 per cent with a total average of 19.66 per cent of consumer's price. Transport charges in rice marketing are not much significant except in case of Nutan bazar to Agartala, which is comparatively high. However, processing charges, which include milling, boiling, cleaning, etc. considerably contribute to total price. Other marketing expenses like packing, commission to local touts, tolls, rent, storage etc. are relatively low in case of marketing from Sonamura to Agartala. These figures are estimated in relation to 40 transactions made from each sample markets to Agartala market.

Table 5.2 shows the vegetable marketing costs and margins involved in marketing process from the five regulated markets to the terminal market at Agartala. It is shown in the table that the farmer's share in the consumer's price in these markets lies between 44.38 to 54.63 per cent with a total average of 50.13 per cent only. Therefore, it can be stated that nearly 50 per cent of every rupee in price goes to marketing set up including transportation cost. Wholesaler's margin lies between 15.00 and 23.07 per cent (total average 17.53 per cent).

Table 5.1: Average Marketing Costs and Margins Involved in Transactions of Rice in Simple Regulated markets to Terminal Markets

(in percentage)

ITEMS	*REGULATED MARKETS TO AGARTALA*					
	Bishal-garh	*Sona-mura*	*Garjee Bazar*	*Nutan*	*Kulai*	*Average*
0	*1*	*2*	*3*	*4*	*5*	*6*
1) Processing Charges (Milling/boiling/ cleaning etc.)	7.58	6.82	5.42	5.62	6.25	6.34
2) Transportation Charges	1.72	2.04	2.87	3.12	2.50	2.45
3) Loading, Unloading and other Labour charges including shortage & waste.	1.52	1.41	1.36	1.00	1.25	1.31
4) Other marketing expenses (Packing/ commission/tolls etc.)	1.98	1.01	1.02	1.62	1.56	1.43
5) Miller's and/or wholesaler's Margin	6.15	6.86	9.53	8.00	7.75	7.66
6) Retailer's Margin	10.50	9.80	13.75	14.82	11.13	12.00
7) Farmer's Share	70.55	72.06	66.05	65.82	69.56	68.81
8) Consumer's Price	100	100	100	100	100	100
Based on number of Transaction	40	40	40	40	40	40

Source : Field Study.

Another feature in case of vegetable marketing is the presence of local arhyatdar or commission agent who collects vegetables either from the markets or directly from the farmers. He maintains liaison between the wholesaler and the farmer. His average estimated margin is 5.50 per cent in Bishalgarh,

4.00 per cent in Sonamura market, 9.94 per cent in Garjee market, 8.74 per cent in Nutan Bazar market and 9.11 per cent in Kulai market. On an average the retailer's margin is estimated as 19.97 per cent in consumer price. Middlemen's share in

Table 5.2: Average Marketing Costs and Margins Involved in Transactions of Vegetables in Sample Regulated Markets to Terminal Markets

(in percentage)

ITEMS	*REGULATED MARKETS TO AGARTALA*					
	Bisha-lgarh	*Sona-mura*	*Garjee Bazar*	*Nutan*	*Kulai*	*Average*
0	*1*	*2*	*3*	*4*	*5*	*6*
1) Transportation charges	1.80	2.03	1.98	2.07	3.96	2.37
2) Loading, Unloading and other Labour Charges including shortage & waste	1.03	1.41	0.79	0.94	0.98	1.03
3) Other Marketing Expenses (Packing/ commission /tolls etc.)	1.53	1.83	1.19	1.80	1.22	1.51
4) Local Arhyatdar's Margin	5.50	4.00	9.94	8.74	9.11	7.46
5) Wholesaler's margin	15.00	16.42	17.41	23.07	15.77	17.53
6) Retailer's Margin	21.22	19.68	21.05	19.00	18.90	19.97
7) Farmer's Share	53.92	54.63	47.64	44.38	50.06	50.13
8) Consumer's Price	100	100	100	100	100	100
Based on number of Transaction	119	119	119	119	119	119

Source: Field Study.

consumer price thus comes to nearly 44.96 per cent of consumer's price. Transportation charges are comparatively high in case of Kulai. Marketing expenses including rent, tolls, packing etc. lie between 1.19 and 1.83 per cent of consumer's price, while loading, unloading and other labour charges are between 0.94 and 1.41 per cent of consumer's price. The estimation are based on 119 transactions in each markets.

Table 5.3 depicts the average fruit marketing costs and margin involved in transactions in sample-regulated markets to the terminal market. The figures are in relation to 110 transactions in each market. The table shows that the farmer's share in consumer's price on an average is 34.63 per cent varying between 27.20 per cent and 45.79 per cent among the selected regulated markets. On the other hand, middleman's margin (karbari / wholesaler and retailer's margin together) is 58.35 per cent. It is to be mentioned that on an average only one third of the consumer's price go to the farmer while the middleman's margin is much higher than the farmer's share.

It is worthwhile to mention that the share of the cultivators in non-tribal dominated markets are on an average, better in comparison to tribal dominated markets. The farmer's share in case of rice marketing in tribal dominated markets varies between 65.82 per cent to 69.56 while in non-tribal dominated market it is found 70.55 per cent to 72.06 per cent. In case of fruit and vegetable marketing, the picture is not different. Thus it indicates the absence of sound marketing set up in tribal dominated markets. Lack of market information, presence of local touts and different type of middlemen, insurgency problems etc. in tribal dominated markets are the probable causes for difference in farmer's share.

In the marketing of agricultural produces the farmer has been the price taker in all cases. Therefore, if the farmer's share in the consumer price is inadequate he will not be encouraged for further production. However, it appears from the above mentioned tables that the cultivators are deprived of adequate margin in consumer price. It is noticed that the rice farmers of the sample regulated markets get comparatively better margin in consumer price followed by vegetable farmers and fruit farmers. In case of rice marketing in sample regulated markets it is seen that the farmer's share in consumer price is around 69 per cent, which speaks of the presence of comparatively strong marketing set up. While, in case of vegetable marketing

Table 5.3: Average Fruits Marketing Costs and Margins Involved in Transactions of Fruits in Sample Regulated Markets to Terminal Market.

(in percentage)

ITEMS	*REGULATED MARKETS TO AGARTALA*					
	Bishal-garh	*Sona-mura*	*Garjee Bazar*	*Nutan*	*Kulai*	*Average*
0	*1*	*2*	*3*	*4*	*5*	*6*
1) Transportation charges	0.98	2.68	3.25	3.35	4.90	3.03
2) Loading, Unloading and other Labour charges including shortage & waste	1.09	1.00	1.97	1.49	1.31	1.37
3) Other Marketing Expenses (Packing/ commission /tolls etc.)	2.04	2.63	3.18	2.82	2.44	2.62
4) Wholesaler's and/ or Karbari's margin	20.00	23.24	25.15	22.14	24.30	22.97
5) Retailer's Margin	30.10	31.50	36.60	43.00	35.70	35.38
6) Farmer's Share	45.79	38.95	29.85	27.20	31.35	34.63
7) Consumer's Price	100	100	100	100	100	100
Based on number of Transaction	110	110	110	110	110	110

Source: Field Study.

it is found that the farmer's share is around 50 per cent, and in that of fruit marketing it is only 34.63 per cent. Comparatively better share of cultivators in the consumer price of rice may be attributed to commercial production, govt. policy, locally suited quality, market arrivals of rice from other states with higher transportation cost due to its geographical location, etc. In this context it may be mentioned that most of the necessary goods are supplied to the sample regulated markets from the terminal market (Agartala) by the only mode of transportation i.e. trucks and small vans. These transporters often have to return empty and at times are hired by traders or cultivators of rice at a nominal charge. It is observed during the field survey in sample markets that other major food grain produces and cash crops are marketed in exchange of inadequate farmer's margin under unfavourable market conditions.

The cultivator's poor economic condition resulting in distress sale of agricultural produces is perhaps the foremost cause of defective marketing, particularly in case of fruit and vegetable marketing. It may be mentioned that out of total 3.18,212 operational holdings in the state, there are 2,16,826 marginal holding (i.e. below 1.00 hectare) and 69,217 small holding (i.e. between 1.00 and 2.00hectares). On the other hand there are only 166 large holding (i.e above 10 hectares) in the state. Thus, it implies that sale of agricultural produces in rural markets of Tripura are dominated by marginal and small cultivators. Moreover, commercial production of agricultural produces like fruits and vegetables except a few are still lacking in rural areas. Therefore, it is very difficult to identify any particular market for any specific produce on a large scale and commercial basis. Thus collection of produces from different locality involves local arhyatdars or agents which further deduct consumer's price.

6

Estimation of Rice Requirement in Tripura

SECTION I

The economy of Tripura is mainly based on agriculture, which contributes 28 per cent of the State's Domestic Product (SDP). Food grains contribute 91.7 per cent of the total cropped area of the State in 2000-2001.Among the food grains, rice is the main cereal produced in the State in terms of production and cropped area. The contributions of other food grains in agricultural sector of the State are insignificant. In spite of some policy measures and application of modern techniques, the shortage of food-grains in the State has been witnessed for a long period and has become a permanent feature of the State economy. In this situation future food grain requirement of the State in terms of rice requirement cannot be ignored but requires attention.

The users of the population data sometimes need the information about future population to make future plans and policy decisions. Projections of future population helps the policy makers by providing magnified image of the consequences of current trends and guide them for taking appropriate actions. Estimation of food-grain requirements of a nation, region or State is one such area where population projection is required .The quantity of food requirements at any point of time depends on the size of the population and these two are positively associated.

The present chapter is planned and designed in this backdrop: The chapter is divided into five sections including the present one. The objectives, methodology, and data sources are discussed in section two. Sections three and four deal with the findings of population projection and rice requirements of the State respectively. Few concluding remarks are put forth in section five.

SECTION II

To understand the basic need of population projection an attempt has been made to project the population of Tripura and to estimate the food grains requirements of the State. Thus the main object of the present paper is (i) to estimate the future population growth of the State for the year 2006 and forthcoming years 2011, 2016 and 2021 and (ii) to estimate the rice requirement of the State for the respective years mentioned above.

To project the population of Tripura the data of the two censuses namely 1991 census and 2001 census are considered. Linear growth function, Geometric growth function and Exponential growth function are taken into consideration for estimation of population growth and the projection is based on the assumption that future conditions affecting the vital processes of the population remain unchanged throughout the period of projection. The process of interpretation determines the projected populations of the intermediate years i.e. between census years.

The I.C.M.R. Advisory Committee (1981) have assessed the caloric requirement in India in three different levels- Physiological level (2150Kcal) retail or home level (2400Kcal) and production level (2700Kcal).The daily per capita cereal requirements as estimated by I.C.M.R. Advisory Committee being 396 g at physiological level, 436 g at retail or home level and 490 g at production level. The estimation at retail level is obtained from physiological level by adding extra 10 per cent cereal due to wastage in kitchen or food given to pets etc. The estimation at production level is worked out from retail level by adding additional 12.5 per cent due to losses in storage and transportation. Rice is the main cereal consumed in Tripura.To provide daily 2400Kcal per head the rice production should be 490 g per caput so that 436 g per capita are available at home level consumption. It cannot be denied that the availability of fat and and milk is far below the levels recommended by I.C.M.R. Advisory Committee. On the other hand in daily diet cereals are the cheapest sources of calorie. So to overcome the caloric deficiency and under nutrition it is essential to consider daily per capita rice production to 670gm so that 600gm per capita are available at retail or home level consumption (Practical Nutrition Target suggested by M. Swaminathan). Thus Swaminathan's model is also taken for consideration in estimation of food-grains requirement of Tripura.

Following the recommendations of I.C.M.R. Advisory Committee and Swaminathan's model the projected requirement of rice production have been worked out. Estimated population of the State, based on exponential growth function has been converted into equivalent adult consumers of food-grains by I.C.A.R. conversion techniques.

SECTION III

According to the 1991 census and 2001 census the population of the State Tripura was 2,757,205 and 3,191,168 respectively. The growth being 01.47% (geometric) and 01.46% (exponential).If the rate be continued further then we cannot exclude another doubling of the population of Tripura by the middle of the present century. The same result is observed in case of world population too by UN Projection (1996).

Again using the information on population size of Tripura in 1991 and 2001 the projected population for 2006, 2011, 2016 and 2021 have been computed and presented in Table 6.1

The table depicts the population projection of Tripura under different growth models namely linear growth model, geometric growth model and exponential growth model. It is observerved that the use of different growth functions yields almost the same estimate of the future population of the State.

Table 6.1: Projected Growth of Population in Tripura (2006, 2011, 2016 and 2021)

Year	*Linear growth function*	*Geometric growth function*	*Exponential growth function*
2001(Actual)	31,91,168	31,91,168	31,91,168
2006	34,42,313	34,,42,223	34,42,357
2011	36,93,458	36,93,277	36,93,546
2016	39,84,133	39,83,833	39,84,279
2021	42,74,808	42,74,389	42,75,012

The table shows that the projection of population for 2006 are 34,42,313; 34,42,223 and 34,42,357 under linear, geometric and exponential growth function respectively. The projection for 2011 vary from a maximum of 3,693,546 persons provide by exponential function to a minimum of 3,693,277 persons obtained by using geometric growth law. The range of variation being 269 persons. The projected population for 2016 under linear, geometric and exponential growth models being 39,84,133; 39,83,833, and 39,84,279 respectively. Lastly the projection of 2021vary from a maximum of 4,257,012 persons provided by the exponential growth law to a minimum of 4,274,389 persons provided by the geometric growth law. The difference is only 623 persons. It appears from the table that the differences between the estimates of projected population obtained by various growth functions are not quite noticeable rather negligibly small. So any estimate under any model may be taken as the estimate of future population size of the State for the respective tears under study. For the sake of simplicity we may consider the estimates 34,42,357; 36,93,546; 39,84,279; and 42,75,012 obtained by using exponential growth law. As the projected population of Tripura during the years

2006, 2011, 2011 and 2021 respectively. Thus if the growth rate of the state's population experienced during 1991-2001 to be constant up to 2021, an increase of some 502,378 people, equivalent to about population size in 1941 of the State, can be expected between 2001 and 2011.also an increase of additional 581,466 persons, equivalent to about 1951-population size of the State, can be expected between 2011 and 2021.

Table 6.2 depicts the expected annual rice requirements for the people of Tripura as per I.C.M.R.Advisory Committee's recommendation and practical nutrition target suggested by Swaminathan, M. The table describes that the growth of population as well the rice requirements to feed the people of the State are increasing continually. It is observed that following the recommendation of I.C.M.R. Advisory Committee, the rice requirement of Tripura in 2001 being 4,75,660 tons in the production level. The table also describes that the rice requirements can be expected to be 5,13,100 tons in 2006; 5,50,540 tons in 2011; 5,93,880 tons in 2016 and in 2021 it can be expected to reach to 6,37,210 tons in the production level so that adequate quantity of rice could be availed at the home level of consumption.

Table 6.2: Projected Rice Requirements in Tripura, (2006, 2011, 2016 and 2021)

Year	*Population*	*Adult Equivalent Consumers*	*Requirements*	
			Rice (Tons)	
			Production Level(a)	*Production Level(b)*
2001	31,91,168(Actual)	26,59,551	4,75,660	6,50,390
2006	34,42,357	28,68,895	5,13,100	7,01,590
2011	36,93,546	30,78,238	5,50,540	7,52,780
2016	39,84,279	33,20,538	5,93,880	8,12,040
2021	42,75,012	35,62,838	6,37,210	8,71,290

Recommended dietary intakes for Indians (1981), I.C.M.R., New Delhi.
Practical Nutrition Target, Swaminathan, M.

SECTION IV

Further the table indicates that following the practical nutrition target suggested by Swaminathan M. the rice requirements of the State can be expected to be 6,50,390 tons in 2001; 7,01,590 tons in 2006; 7,52,780 tons in 2001; 8,12,040 tons in 2016 and 8,71,290 tons in 2021 respectively.

Now it is a fact that majority of the people in Tripura are not only the consumers of rice but are also habituated to intake rice even more that two times daily. Also a good number of people usually intake more rice due to poor economic condition. They are unable to include fat and milk products in their diet upto the standard as prescribed by I.C.M.R. Advisory Committee. In addition, majority of the population generally reside in the rural ares.Under such circumstances the estimates derived by Swaminathatn's guideline may be considered as the more practical and reliable.

In 2001 the expected rice requirement of the State being 6, 50,390 tons in the production level where as the actual production was 5,13,402 tons. Thus a difference of 1,36,988 tons of rice equivalent to 27 per cent of the actual production of rice during 2000-2001 were needed to meet the demand of food security in terms of rice of the State. In order to examine the impact of projected population on the rice requirement of the State let us assume that the actual production of rice during 2000-2001 be continued. Under this consideration, in addition to the existing level of production of rice an extra 1,88,188 tons of rice equivalent to 37 per cent of the existing production are to be needed in 2006. In 2011 it will be 47 per cent (2,39,378 tons) of the assumed existing level of production of rice. In 2016, an additional 58 per cent or 2,98,638 tons are to be produced for self sufficiency. Lastly in 2021 additional to the existing production figure an additional 3,57,888 tons of rice equivalent to 70 per cent of the existing production will be expected to feed the entire population of the State.

SECTION V

In conclusion it may be stated that between 1991 and 2001 the population of a Tripura increased by about 4.33 lakh. The exponential growth rate being ¼ per cent assuming the growth rate to be constant up to 2021 an increase of some 502,378 person can be expected between 2001 and 2011.This would be equivalent to about the population size of the State in 1941 between 2011 and 2021 an additional 581,466 persons would be added afresh. If the growth rate observed during 1991-2001, continues then Tripura would face another doubling of the population by middle of the present century.

It is observed in the study that the present rice production of the State has to be increased by 47 per cent in 2011, 58 per cent 2016 and 70 per cent in 2021 respectively for self sufficiency. Otherwise Tripura has to depend upon the other States for its requirement of rice for consumption. On the other hand it will not be an exaggeration to conclude that during coming decades the impact of projected population on the food scarcity in terns of rice requirement of the State will be reached to an alarming position.

REFERENCES

Bhende, Asha A. Kanitkar, Tara (2001): *Principles of Population Studies,* Himalaya Publishing House, Mumbai.

Cox, Peter R (1970): *Demography,* Cambridge.

Directorate of Statistics,Government of Tripura; *Some Basic Statistics of Tripura* (Various issues)

Hans Raj (1999): *Fundamentals of Demography,* Surjeet Publications.

ICAR: *Human Nutrition vis-à-vis Animal Nutrition in India.*

ICMR Advisory Committee (1981): *Recommended Dietary Intakes for Indians,* Indian Council for Medical Research, New Delhi.

Mishra, B.D (1995): *An Introduction to the Study of Population,* South Asian Publishers Pvt. Ltd, New Delhi.

Nathan, Keyfitz (1977): *Applied Mathematical Demography,* John Wiley and Sons, New York.

Pollard, A.H ; Yusuf, Farhar; and Polland, G.N (1981); *Demographic Techniques,* Pergamon Press.

Srivastava, O.S (1998): *Demography and Population Studies,* Vikas Publishing House Pvt. Ltd.

Swaminathan, M (1997): Essentials of Food and Nutrition, Val-11. The Bangalore Printing and Publishing Co. Ltd, Bangalore United Nations (1996): *World Population Assessment and Projection.*

7

Development of Small Scale Industries in Tripura

Tripura is one of the seven States of the North-Eastern region of India. About 83 per cent of its population live in rural areas and hence. The economy of the State is basically dominated by the primary sector. As far as industrialization is concerned the State is yet to emerge out of industrial backwardness. The overall backwardness of the State is evident from the composite infrastructural index evolve by the Centre for Monitoring Indian Economy (CMIE) based on the availability of power, irrigation, road, railways, post-office, education, health and banking. As per the CMIE index Tripura is the second most backward State in the country.

The process of setting up large and medium scale industries in the State is not satisfactory due to several constraints like undulating topography, limited size of market, lack of skilled and semi-skilled manpower, inadequate infrastructure, low level of per capita income, insurgency problems and so on. At present there are only two large and medium scale industries in the State. Development of small scale industries (SSI) therefore is the only alternative to the problems that need immediate solutions viz. mobilization of local resources, unemployment, dispersal of industrial activity and amore equitable distribution of the income. Importance of small sector in removing economic backwardness of a State like Tripura lies in its significance for generation of employment with low capital cost. Moreover, small-scale industries are adaptable to rural and semi–urban areas where infrastructure has not been fully developed. Therefore, it is not an exaggeration to say that small scale industry should be assigned a pivotal role in the scheme of industrialization and economic development of the State. The present article focuses upon the issues associated with the development of small-scale sector in Tripura. The article has five sections including the present one. Growth and Status of SSI in Tripura is discussed in section two. Strategy for development and potential areas for development are discussed in section three and four respectively. Finally a few concluding remarks are put forward in section five.

Growth and Status of SSI

In spite of vast scope, the development of SSI in Tripura still remains at a very nascent stage. However, as a result of a few policy measure taken and support provided like financial and technical, the SSI sector has grown considerably in the recent years. Yet it is minimum in the context of regional or national growth rate.

Table 7.1: Principal Characteristics of Industries in Tripura (1955-56 and 1965-66)

	1955-56	*1965-66*
Number of Industries	25	49
Number of Industrial Units	5133	3695
Number of Workers Engaged	10438	13626
Fixed Capitals (Rs.)	24,06,565	95,13,000
Working Capital (Rs)	6,69,122	48,38,000
Fixed Capital per unit (Rs)	468.84	2574.56
Working Capital per unit (Rs)	130.36	1309.34
Employment per Industrial Unit	2.03	3.69

Sources: 1) Techno-Economic Survey of Tripura, NCAER, New Delhi, 1961.

2) Report of the fact-finding Survey of Tripura, UBI, Calcutta, 1970.

Principal characteristics of industries during early plan periods of Tripura are depicted in Table 7.1. The information of 1955-56 is based on data of Techno-Economic Survey of Tripura, NCAER, New Delhi. 1965-66 data relates to Report of the Fact – Finding Survey of Tripura, UBI, Calcutta. The table reveals that there were 25 industries in 1955-56 which increased to 49 in 1965-66. Number of workers engaged has also been increased from 10,438 to 13,626 during the period. These two reports indicate the diversification and mordernisation of industrial structure of Tripura. The reports also indicate that in spite of modernization, traditional industries of the State constitute the lion share.

Table 7.2: Principal Characteristics of Registered Small Scale Industries in Tripura

Number of registered working units	812
Number of reporting units	809
Employment (Nos.)	10,069
Fixed Investment (Rs. Lakh)	1,473
Gross value of production in 1987-88 (Rs. Lakh)	2,957
Units located in rural area	365
Units located in urban area	444
units registered under Factories Act	190
Number of proprietary units	716
Number of partnership units	68
Number of units engaged in manufacturing Activities.	438
Number of units engaged in processing Activities.	130
Number of units not consumed energy	125
Number of exporting units.	17

Source :- Directorate of Industries, Government of Tripura. The Second All India Census of Registered Small Scale Industries, Tripura State.

Table 7.3: Small Scale Industries in Tripura (1971-72 and 1987-88)

Industry	*Number of Units*		*Employment (Number)*	
	1971-72	*1987-88*	*1971-72*	*1987-88*
Wood products	41	99	314	799
Metal Products	51	62	250	464
Repair Services	26	86	129	394
Rubber & Plastic Products	21	95	60	298
Paper products & printing	1	51	11	267
Chemical Products	6	18	154	158
Metal products (Basic Metal & Alloy)	3	5	19	110
Machinery and parts	17	23	127	56
Electrical machinery	5	19	16	51
Hosiery & Garments	3	5	10	28
Misc. manufacturing industries.	5	6	9	20
Transport. Equipment		4		18
Leather products	2	5	11	17
Other services		3		15
Beverage & Tobacco		3		9
Non-metallic mineral product	8	78	256	4998
Food products	37	247	323	2367
	246	809	1698	10069

Source: 1) Directorate of Industries, Government of Tripura, The 2nd All India Census of Registered Small Scale Industries, Tripura State.

2) Basic statistics of the North Eastern Region, NEC, Shillong, 1977 and 1982.

Table 7.4: Registered Small Scale Industries in Tripura (1997-98 to 200-01)

(Rs. in Lakh)

Name of District	*1997-98*		*1998-1999*		*1999-2000*		*2000-2001*	
	Unit	*Investment*	*Unit*	*Investment*	*Unit*	*Investment*	*Unit*	*Investment*
West	1704	398.5	1747	323.4	1785	272.8	1804	389.1
North	421	301.8	435	150.8	445	71.31	454	406.6
South	292	10.7	295	32.3	309	45.04	310	6.00
Dhalai	7	64.6	11	43.1	11	43.1	14	5.05
Total	2424	774.6	2488	549.6	2547	432.2	2582	806.75

Source: *Economic Review*, 2000-01, Directorate of Economics and Statistics, Government of Tripura.

Table 7.5: Numbers of Registered Factories in Tripura

Year	*Under Sec.2m (i)*	*Under Sec. 2m (ii)*	*Under Sec. 25*	*Total Factories*
1981	97	77	44	218
1990	173	244	593	1010
1991	163	172	647	982
1992	174	167	751	1092
1993	193	169	766	1128
1994	201	150	800	1151
1995	208	136	829	1173
1996	226	125	860	1211
1997	223	111	895	1229
1998	244	119	935	1298
1999	250	121	960	1331
2000	252	130	967	1349
2007	317	129	1055	1555

Source: Factories of Boilers Organisation, Government of Tripura.

Principal characteristics of Registered Small Scale Industries based on Second All India Census of Registered SSI, Tripura State are shown in Table 7.2 According to that census report there were 809 reporting units with employment of 10,069 person. The numbers of units engaged in manufacturing activities are 438 and the numbers of units engaged in processing activities are 130 as on that data. Another interesting feature is there were 17 exporting units in the State.

Various types of SSI industries in Tripura (1971-72 and 1987-88) are shown in Table 7.3. It is evident from the Table that the metal products have the highest number of units followed by wood products, food products, chemical products etc. during the year 1971-72. While food products have the highest number of units followed by wood products, rubber and plastic, non- metallic, mineral products etc. during the period 1987-88. There were 1698 person employed in 1971-72 and 10, 069 people in 1987- 88 in these SSI units.

The numbers of units and their investment during 1997-98 and 2000-2001 have been depicted in Table 7.4. During this period the number of units have increased from 2424 to 2582 units. Investments in SSI have also increased from 775.8 Lakhs to 806.7 lakhs. West district of Tripura has the highest number of SSI units followed by North, South and Dhalai. The number of registered factories in Tripura during the period 1981 to 2000 is presented in Table 7.5. During this period the number of factories have increased from 218 to 1349.

Strategy for Development

In the face of acute poverty and rising unemployment in the State the pressing need for rapid economic development has led the State government to spell out its policies and programmes in favour of industrialisation. In the process of achieving such rapid industrialisation, the growth of sickness in SSI units is causing a severe strain on the economic system of the State. The phenomenon of sickness not only tended to aggravate the problem of unemployment, but also rendered infractuous capital investment and consequently created an adverse climate for further industrial growth.

Revival of potential sick units is perhaps the foremost task. But uniform guidelines or parameters for revival of sick units, delay in decision making particularly by banks and TIDC in rehabilitation cases, absence of standard documentation of rehabilitation facilities etc. act as impediments in the process of revival of sick units. The main impediment to development of SSI is perhaps the non-viability of many units, which are started without much consideration to the resource endowments in the State and eventually turn sick. It is mentioned earlier that 99 per cent of total sick units are non viable in the State. Therefore, potential areas for development of SSI should be identified.

Potential Areas of Development

It is not an exaggeration to say that SSI should be assigned a pivotal role in the scheme of industrialization and economic development of the State. In spite of various measures taken by the State government, there has not been any significant improvement in the scenario. Survey of industrial potential in the State was first made by the National Council of Applied Economic Research (NCAER). It classified the potential industries of Tripura into: (a) processing industries, (b) engineering industries, (c) wood based industries, (d) leather industries. Another similar survey was conducted in the year 1970 by a Joint Institutional Study Team consisting of the representatives of the RBI, IDBI, ICICI and the IFC. The Plan Evaluation Organisation of the Government of Tripura also made a survey of the SSI units in two industrial estates located at Agartala (Arundhutinagar) and Udaipur in 1975. Thereafter Entrepreneurship Development Institute of India (Project opportunities in Tripura, 1992), North Eastern Industrial Consultants Ltd. (Report on Prospects and Possibilities of setting up Industrial estates in Manipur, Mizoram and Tripura,1995) and Tripura Industrial Development corporation (Industrial

Potential Survey in Tripura, 1998-99) have made the industrial survey in the State.

The natural resources, favourable agro-climatic conditions and traditionally skilful manpower available in the State reasonably advocates setting up of SSI units based on these resources and compatible with these conditions and circumstances (EDII, 1992). The Shivaraman committee suggested that in the north-eastern region, small scale industries based on locally available natural resources and industries capable of meeting growing local needs might be promoted. Considering the marketability and manpower ability, demand pattern and the existing constraints the most appropriate areas for small scale industries may be identified as follows: (i) forest based, (ii) agro based, (iii) livestock based, and (iv) gas based and (v) service sector based. Therefore the State government needs to revamp its industrial policy and concentrate more on setting up industries based upon these (Chakraborty, 2004).

Tripura is endowed with dense forests, occupying an area of about 606168 hect. And accounting for more than 58 per cent of the total geographical area. Out of the total forest resources in the State only 30.22 per cent is in actual use, leaving large areas potentially exploitable. Value of outturn forest product in Tripura was Rs. 137,65000 in the year 2000-2001. The forests are rich in timber, bamboo, cane, agar-wood, grasses and medicinal herbs. Thus the forests may provide raw materials to a number of small scale industries based on these resources.

In natural rubber production, Tripura ranks second only to Kerala in the country. More and more plantations are reaching yielding stage and the productivity levels are also encouraging. In view of the area under plantations together with the growth potential and rubber production trends, the State has been identified as the second rubber capital of the country. There is a vast potential for setting up of rubber-based industries in the State. The rubber produced in the State is also of high quality which faces trading problems in the absence of any rubber based industry in the State. In 2002-2003 an area of about

17,701 hectare land was under natural rubber plantation in the State. Total rubber production was 17,849 MT and total value of rubber production was Rs.69.42 crores in 2002-03. The raw rubber now produced is being sent out to the neighbouring States for further value addition. This can easily be done in the State through development of rubber based SSI units.

Agriculture, in the State, also can play an important role in industrial development. It provides raw materials to a number of small scale and cottage industries. Cash crops and spices with commercial potentiality like sugarcane, jute, mesta, cotton etc. are being successfully cultivated in the State. Citronella, an aromatic crop has emerged as an important crop with industrial potentials. Production of essential oils from various species of herbs grown in the State may lead to development of industries like cosmetic, perfumery and pharmaceutical products. The State also produces a variety of fruits. The marketable surplus of these is enough for opening up more fruit processing industries in the State as revealed by a study conducted by North-Eastern Council. Production of high value, low volume items like pepin from papaya or pectin from citrus peel is pertinent for horticulture based SSI units in the State.

The agro-climatic conditions are favourable for growing various fruit and horticultural crops. The products of Tripura are well known- both in raw as well as processed form . There is scope for expansion of area under any specific variety, if required. A modern Food Processing Technology Park is being set up near Agartala, to give a fillip to this sector. An Agri Export Zone for Pineapple is also being developed. There is a vast potential for setting up of food processing units in the State. Seasonal fruits such as pineapples, jackfruits, oranges, litchis etc. are grown in large quantities. The processed fruits can also be exported to Bangladesh.At present large quantities of fruits are informally traded with Bangladesh from Tripura.

Cashewnut, areca nut and coconut are widely produced in Tripura. Small industry has scope to develop based on these cash crops particularly coconut which is abundantly grown in the State (3183 MT in 2000-2001) in an area of 8370 hectares. Processing of coconut may give rise to many industries like coir, rope, mat carpet, oil etc. The industries based on coconut is highly employment oriented also.

Handloom and handicrafts are other potential areas for SSI units. At present handloom is the largest industry in Tripura There are about 1.25 lakh handlooms employing about one lakh weavers in the State. Unfortunately only 9000 handlooms are in commercial operation which cannot meet the requirements of the State. Therefore, there is wide scope to develop handloom industries in the small scale sector. Inspite of locality available resources and manpower the handicrafts industry of Tripura is not up to the expectation due to several problems. At present there are about 5000 craftsman engaged in producing different varieties of handicrafts. However as the State has long been known for its traditional skill in bamboo and cane work, the handicrafts industry has wide scope for development including export to other countries.

Tripura also has immense potential for live stock, poultry and fishery. The State not only has the required agro climatic conditions but also all the resources necessary for increased animal production. According to various live stock census there are adequate number of live stock and poultry in the State. These may cater to develop SSI units in the related areas.

Conclusion

In Tripura about 84 per cent of the people live in rural areas and more than 70 per cent of the population depend for their livelihood in agriculture and allied activities. In such a situation development of industrial sector must be related to agriculture and allied activities. Before taking any strategy plan, it is also necessary to evaluate the performance of the existing SSI units and also to analyse the potentiality of expansion of market in the State or region itself and outside the region.

Tripura lags behind in economic development due to her poor infrastructural facilities. However, Tripura has immense reserves of gas which can generate power so essential for industrial , agricultural and commercial development . The State is endowed with natural gas reserves of 588 billion cu. M. which has huge potentiality to generate power in excess of Tripura's requirement. Recently the North Eastern Electric Power Corporation (NEEPCO) and other organizations have initiated setting up of gas based power projects with 500 MW capacity .If the target is achieved, Tripura will have a surplus in power generation .In the absence of any industrial base in the State Tripura can easily export the excess power to Bangladesh and neighbouring regions.

Finally development strategy for backward State requires simultaneous action on various fronts for increasing employment opportunities, production and productivity. Agriculture, needless to mention, being the largest single source of income and employment in Tripura, takes precedence over other activities in the State. Development of agriculture, however, is, to a limited extent, development upon the development of the infrastructure, tertiary sector and rural industries. Cottage and village industries in Tripura have traditionally provided substantial employment opportunities to rural people of the State. These are traditional occupation of various artisan classes in the village of the State. Cane and bamboo, village pottery, village oil gur and khandeswary, bee keeping, processing of cereal and pulses, etc. are a few of those available in rural areas of the State. These industries having forward linkage with agriculture, provide considerable scope for increased production and employment. Therefore, strategy should be formulated to odernize these industries with an aim to make them more economically viable for competition.

REFERENCES

Agarwal, A.K. (1988): *North Eastern Economy Problem and prospects,* Mittal Publications, New Delhi.

Bhattacherjee, P.R. (1993): *Economic Transaction in Tripura,* Vikas Publishing, New Delhi.

Chakraborty, Kiran Sankar & Pramanik A.K. (1999): Sickness in Small Scale Industries of North-Eastern Region, *Southern Economist,* November 1.

Chakraborty, Kiran Sankar (2002): Sickness in Small Scale Industries of Tripura, *Vidyasagar University Journal of Commerce,* vol.7, Midnapur.

Chakraborty, Kiran Sankar (2004) : Structural Change and Strategy of Development – Resource-Industry Linkages in Tripura, in *'Structural change and strategy of development'*, Gurudas Das (ed.), Akansha Publications , New Delhi .

Chakraborty, Kiran Sankar and Das, B.C. (2002): An insight into the development of SSI in Tripura, *Southern Economist,* Vol-41, No-8, Bangalore.

Entrepreneurship Development Institute of India (1992): *Project Opportunities in Tripura,* Gujarat.

Government of Tripura, Directorate of Economics and Statistics: *Economic Review,* Various Issues.

Government of Tripura, Directorate of Economics and Statistics: *Statistical Abstract,* Various Issues.

Government of Tripura, Evaluation Organisation (1975): *Evaluation Report on Industrial Estates in Tripura.*

Government of Tripura, Directorate of Industries: *The Second All India Census of Registered Small Scale Industries.*

Government of Tripura, Directorate of Industries: *Tripura Incentive Scheme,* 1995.

Government of Tripura, Tripura Industrial Development Corporation (1998-99): Industrial Potential Survey in Tripura Prepared by TCS.

Government of Tripura, Tripura Industrial Development Corporation (2001): *Investment Opportunities and Industrial Infrastructure in Tripura.*

Mali, D.D. and Deka, P. (1987): *Industrial Development in North-East India,* Omson Publications, Guwahati.

Nagaiya: *Small Industry Development in India. Policy, Programmes and Institutional Support,* NISIET, Hyderabad.

National Council of Applied Economic Research (1961): *Techno Economic Survey of Tripura,* New Delhi.

North Eastern Council: *Basic Statistics of North Eastern Region,* 2004, Shillong.

North Eastern Council: *Toward Regional Development Plans and Perspective,* Publication No. 8, Jan. 1980, Shillong.

North Eastern Industrial Consultants Ltd. (1995): Report on Prospects and Possibilities of setting up Industrial Estates in Manipur, Nagaland, Mizoram and Tripura for IDBI, Agartala.

United Bank of India (1970): *Report of the Fact-finding Survey of Tripura,* Calcutta.

8

Sickness in Small Scale Industries of Tripura State

Small enterprises play a crucial role in providing large scale employment opportunities at lower capital costs, establishing a wide industrial base and dispersing industries into rural and backward areas, assuring more equitable distribution of national income and wealth and promoting development of ancillary enterprises that can integrate with large and medium sized industries. The consistent support in all industrial policy resolutions of the Government of India has helped the small scale sector to emerge as a dynamic sector of the economy, accounting for nearly 40 per cent of the gross value of output in the manufacturing sector.

The Government has advanced support to small-scale sector in various forms in terms of fiscal, monetary and institutional mechanisms. As a result of the initiatives taken, the small scale sector, over the years, has proved itself to be an integral part of the Indian economy. The sector contributes a major part of total industrial production and is also a significant foreign exchange earner. According to the Ministry of SSI there are more than 44 lakh units providing 7,500 different items for domestic as well as foreign markets. At present the sector accounts for 95 per cent of industrial units in the country. The sector contributes nearly 6.29 per cent of GDP and 33.97 per cent for national exports. Constant support to SSI sector by the Government in terms of fiscal and monitoring policies have helped this sector to emerge as a dynamic and vibrant sector of Indian economy.

The process of setting up large and medium scale industries in the State is not satisfactory due to several constraints like undulating topography, limited size of market, lack of skilled and semi-skilled manpower, inadequate infrastructure, low level of per capita income, insurgency problems and so on. At present there are only two large and medium scale industrial units in the State. Development of small scale industrial sector (SSI), therefore, is the only alternative to the problems that need immediate solutions viz., mobilisation of local resources, unemployment, dispersal of industrial activity and a more equitable distribution of the income. Importance of small sector in removing economic backwardness of a State lies in its significance for generation of employment with low capital cost. Moreover, small scale industries are adaptable to rural and semi-urban areas where infrastructure has not been fully developed.

While the governments are striving for development of small scale sector, sickness among the SSI units on the other hand, are growing at an alarming rate and threatening to cripple the State economy. The present article highlights the issue of sickness among the SSI units of the State.

Magnitude of Sickness

Combining the three yardsticks used to measure sickness. viz., (a) delay in repayment of loan over one year, (b) decline in net worth by 50% and (c) decline in output in last three years, about 13.98% of the units in the registered SSI sector of our country were identified to be either sick or incipient sick in 3rd All India Census of Small Scale Industries (2001-2002), while this percentage was only 6.89 in the case of unregistered units. In the total SSI sector, this percentage was 7.82.The States of Kerala, Tamil Nadu, Andhra Pradesh, Karnataka and Maharastra had maximum number of stick/incipient sick SSI units. These five States together accounted for 54.28% of the sick/incipiently sick SSI units in the country.

In the face of acute poverty and rising unemployment in Tripura, the pressing need for rapid economic development has led the State government to spell out its policies and programmes in favour of industrialisation. In the process of achieving such rapid industrialisation, the growth of sickness in SSI units is causing a severe strain on the economic system of the State. The phenomenon of sickness not only tended to aggravate the problem of unemployment, but also rendered infructuous capital investment and consequently created an adverse climate for further industrial growth.

The magnitude of the problem is evident from the fact that 52.90 percent of the total units in the State are closed which is fairly high compared to other States of the North-East

Table 8.1: State-wise Percentage of Working/Closed Units in Registered SSI Sector

State	*No.of Working units*	*No. of Closed units*	*Total units*	*% of closed units*	*% of closed to NE Region*
1	2	3	4	5	6
Arunachal Pradesh	255	248	503	49.30	1.51
Assam	14453	10338	24791	41.70	63.05
Manipur	4599	1226	5825	21.05	7.48
Meghalaya	1939	1908	3847	49.60	11.64
Mizoram	2733	1313	4046	32.45	8.01
Nagaland	568	129	697	18.51	0.79
Sikkim	174	155	329	47.11	0.95
Tripura	959	1077	2036	52.90	6.57
N.E. Region	25680	16394	42074	38.96	100.00
All India	1374974	887427	2262401	39.23	-

Source: Final Results, Third All India Census of Small Scale Industries 2001-2002 (DC, SSI)

Region. There are some more working units which are either sick or on the verge of getting so. According to an estimate, 20-25 percent of reported working SSI units in the State are weak (Tripura Industrial Development Corporation, Agartala). It is shown in Table 8.1 that Tripura has the highest percentage of closed units followed by Meghalaya (49.60%), Arunachal Pradesh (49.30%) and Sikkim (47.11%). So far as the number of closed units are concerned, Assam has the highest (10,338) followed by Meghalaya (1908) and Mizoram (1313) respectively. According to an estimate, out of total 6914 sick units in the State, there are only 549 potentially viable sick units and 5693 are non- viable sick units. (Indian Institute of Entrepreneurship, Guwahati).

Table 8.2: State-wise Classification of Sick Small Scale Industrial Units in NER as on 31.03.1999

State	*Potentially viable*	*Non-viable*	*Viability yet to be decided*	*Total sick units*
Arunachal Pradesh	6	102	8	116
Assam	581	9300	705	10586
Manipur	391	4367	79	5237
Meghalaya	21	401	25	447
Mizoram	0	40	0	40
Nagaland	3	160	3	166
Tripura	549	5693	672	6914
Total	1551	20063	1892	23506

Causes of Sickness

According to the 3rd All India Census of Small Scale Industries, 'Lack of demand', 'Shortage of working capital' and 'Marketing problem' were the main reasons for sickness/incipient sickness in both the registered and unregistered SSI sectors.

Table 8.3: Percentage Distribution of Sick/Incipient Sick Units in Total SSI Sector

State	*Sick units (erosion of networth of delayin repayment)*	*Incipient sick units (Continuous decline in gross output)*	*Sick/ Incipient sick Units*	*Sick units asper RBI Criteria*
1	*2*	*3*	*4*	*5*
Arunachal Pradesh	0.02	0.01	0.01	0.02
Assam	1.23	1.01	1.02	0.98
Manipur	0.12	0.53	0.50	0.12
Meghalaya	0.22	0.06	0.08	0.26
Mizoram	0.02	0.01	0.01	0.01
Nagaland	0.01	0.00	0.00	0.01
Sikkim	0.02	0.01	0.01	0.01
Tripura	0.45	0.21	0.20	0.54
India Total	**100.00**	**100.00**	**100.00**	**100.00**

Source: Final Results, Third All India Census of Small Scale Industries 2001-2002 (DC,SSI)

Some of the identified factors are as follows:

i) Frequent changes in the policies, rules and regulations of State government, banks and other financial institutions towards SSI units;

i) Frequent changes in the policies, rules and regulations of State government, banks and other financial institutions towards SSI units;

ii) Absence of adequate railway facilities (only 45 km) and high transportation costs in comparison to other States;

iii) CMIE-evolved composite infrastructure index of Tripura

shows the infrastructural backwardness of the State, resulting longer gestation period and weakness of the supporting services;

iv) Absence of attractive incentive schemes;

v) Unattractive sale tax regulations;

vi) Shortage of power supply in the State. During the year 1998-99 there was 25 MW shortage of power, which was highest among the North-East States. Per capita consumption of power in the State is also low in comparison to the other States of the North-East.

vii) Shortage of skilled workers, efficient managers and above all motivated entrepreneurs;

viii) In comparison to other parts of India, working capital requirement in SSI units of Tripura is more due to infrastructural and geographical barrier resulting in inadequate working capital finance by the funding agencies as they abide by uniform rules.

ix) Frequent blockades of the Assam-Agartala Road (life-line of Tripura) causing uncertainties and shortage of essential raw materials and construction materials;

x) Outdated and inferior techniques of productions resulting in higher cost of production;

xi) Limited market support by the government in the form of unplanned purchases at the end of financial year by the government departments and organisations;

xii) Inadequate modern marketing facilities;

xiii) Disturbed socio-political conditions of the State.

Remedial Measures

Various study groups and experts have identified the basic constraints for the development of SSI units in Tripura. The remedial measures should therefore be framed to remove all such constraints. Any attempt in this respect be viewed at a wider perspective involving the State and central governments, commercial banks, promotional organisations, financial institutions and entrepreneurs. As the State is endowed with abundant resources, entrepreneurs should be induced to set up industries based on these resources. For this, a detailed up to date inventory of available resources in the State will have to be made along with industry wise potential survey of the State. It is also necessary to have a data bank as a source of information accessible to entrepreneurs, which can guide them in decision-making when selecting a new project or for expansion and diversification.

At present there are 10 industrial estates / areas in the State providing 60 industrial sheds, out of which 38 units are working (Government of Tripura, IDBI, 2001). A review of working of various industrial estates in north-eastern region (Status Paper on Industrial Estates by SIET, Guwahati) shows that the primary cause of non-working of many industrial units in industrial estates is the location of the estates. Bodhjungnagar Growth Centre in West District and Dewanpara Integrated Infrastructure Development Centre in North District are the examples. Therefore, the industrial estate should be located in places where other infrastructural facilities (social and economic) are available. And selection of site should be made on the basis of techno economic consideration rather than on political consideration. Level of productivity of SSI units in the State has also to be improved. This is possible only if the entrepreneurs aim at production of quality goods with local resources at the lowest cost. (NECON, 1995).

Many small units of the State have difficulties in marketing their products because they cannot afford the expenses involved in an elaborate marketing set up. Very few SSI units of the State are fortunate to have a committed market close by. It is, thus, necessary to have some organisation to look after the marketing of products manufactured by small units. The State government can encourage the setting up of industry wise marketing organisation in the co-operative or government sector. At present various incentive schemes are available to the SSI units in the State. Central and State governments' package of incentives includes mainly capital investment subsidy, sales tax exemption (5 yrs.), interest subsidy, transport subsidy, and income tax exemption (10 yrs.) (IDBI, 2001 and Department of Industries, Government of Tripura, 1995). According to a study conducted by NEITCO, subsidies are grossly inadequate. Therefore, these need to be enhanced as also some other type of subsidies introduced for accelerating industrial growth.

Entrepreneurs have a severe limitation in terms of their time and expertise. They are to perform various statutory requirements with Industry Department, Labour Department, Sales Tax, Income Tax, ESI, Provident Fund, Factories, Banks, Financial Institutions, etc. There should be a single agency which can help the entrepreneur in dealing with the various government bodies. Such an agency will free the entrepreneurs to concentrate on the critical areas of business.

There should also be another agency in the State which can co-ordinate the various activities pertaining to SSI, namely, promotion of new industries, identification and training of entrepreneurs, preparation of feasibility reports, arrangement of loans from financial institutions, providing consultancy services, monitoring the activities of the units and so on. The above task of 'Single Window' system may be entrusted to the Tripura Industrial Development Corporation Ltd. or to any other similar organisation.

Concluding Remarks

The main impediment to development of SSI units is perhaps the non-viability of many units which are started without much consideration to the resource endowments in the State and eventually turn sick. Revival of potential sick units is, therefore, the foremost task. But the factors like uniform guidelines on parameters for relief for revival of sick units, delay in decision particularly by banks and TIDC in rehabilitation cases, absence of standard documentation of rehabilitation facilities etc. act as impediments in the process of revival of sick units.

9

Indo-Bangladesh Border Trade: Tripura's Perspectives

The geographical location of North-East India (NEI) has a special significance to border trade. The region share a longer border with neighbours such as China, Bangladesh, Bhutan and Myanmar than mainland. Perhaps this is the reason why NEI takes interest in these countries for establishing trade relations. The poor infrastructures of the region, coupled with transportation bottlenecks are the main reasons of non-development. Hence, NEI can take advantage of border trade and generate economic activities because of her close proximity to these countries.

NEI shares 1880 km border with Bangladesh where in, 1439 km is land border and 446 km riverine tract. Assam, Mizoram, Meghalaya and Tripura are the four of the NEI States, which share their border with Bangladesh. Assam has a total of 263 km, Mizoram 318 km, Meghalaya 443 km and Tripura 856 km of border area (both land and riverine) . As can be seen from the Table 9.1, Tripura has the lions share of border area with 773 km of land border and 83 km riverine border which accounts for 45.53 per cent of the total border area of our country with Bangladesh. So far as Indo-Bangla land border is concerned, Tripura shares 53.72 per cent of total land border. It is also to be noted that Tripura and Bangladesh have always shared close racial, lingual, ethnic and cultural affinity. The importance of border trade between the two regions, therefore, cannot be ignored but requires special attention.

Table 9.1: Indo-Bangla Border Area

NE State	*Riverine*	*Land Border*	*Total*	*% in Total*
Tripura	83	773	856	45.53
Meghalaya	-	443	443	23.56
Mizoram	260	58	318	16.91
Assam	103	160	263	13.99
Total	446	1439	1880	100

Source: Government of India website.

The present article focuses upon the issues associated with Indo-Bangla trade relation in Tripura's perspectives. The chapter has six sections including the present one. Section two deals with the present status of trade between Bangladesh and Tripura; section three deals with the potential areas for developing trade between Tripura and Bangladesh. Impediments in the trade relation and strategies for developing trade between the two regions are dealt in sections four and five respectively. Finally the concluding remarks are put forward in section six.

Present Status of Trade

Bilateral trade between India and Bangladesh has been increasing rapidly since the last two decades. However, it is also noted that the balance of trade between the two countries considerably tilts towards India. This may be due to the fact that India's imports from Bangladesh are extremely skewed, limited to only a few commodities, as compared to its exports to Bangladesh. Indo-Bangla trade is currently close to $2 billion. The Indian exports to Bangladesh are nearly $1.8 billion. Hence NEI in general and Tripura in particular with its close proximity to Bangladesh can obviously play a distinct role in this bilateral trade. Let's take a glance on the present status of Tripura's import and export scenario with Bangladesh in comparison to NEI.

It is observed from the Table 9.2 that value of imports from Bangladesh to Tripura is quite high in comparison to NEI. The total value of imports from Bangladesh to Tripura has increased from Rs.7.44 crores in 1999-2000 to Rs.10.18 crore in the year 2003-2004 .While the value of imports from Bangladesh to NEI has increased from Rs.9.43 crores to Rs.11.52 crores during the same period .The share of Tripura in the total imports of NEI during 2003-2004 is 88.37 per cent.

Table 9.2: Status of Value of Imports from Bangladesh to Tripura and NEI

Year	*Value of Imports to TRIPURA (Rs. in crores)*	*Value of Imports to NEI (Rs. in crores)*	*Share of Tripura in value of imports to NEI (Percentage)*
1999-2000	7.44	9.43	78.89
2000-2001	6.16	7.19	85.67
2001-2002	4.38	5.52	79.35
2002-2003	5.47	6.10	89.67
2003-2004	10.18	11.52	88.37
2004-2005	N.A	19.58	N.A

Source: Office of the Central Excise and Land Custom, Government of India, Agartala.

N.A = Not Available.

Table 9.3 shows the value of exports to Bangladesh from Tripura and NEI during the period 1999-2000 and 2004-2005. Here the picture is reverse. The value of exports from Tripura during the reported years is meager in comparison to exports from NEI. The value of exports to Bangladesh from Tripura has declined from Rs.1.74 crores in the year 1999-2000 to Rs.1.35 crores in 2004-2005. On the other hand value of exports from NEI has increased from Rs.169.82 crores to Rs. 238.11 crores in

Table 9.3: Status of Value of Exports from Tripura and NEI to Bangladesh

Year	*Value of Exports from TRIPURA (Rs.in crores)*	*Value of Exports from NEI (Rs. In crores)*	*Share of Tripura in value of exports from NEI (Percentage)*
1999-2000	1.74	169.82	1.02
2000-2001	0.65	151.23	0.42
2001-2002	1.13	185.89	0.60
2002-2003	1.32	202.70	0.65
2003-2004	1.20	238.11	0.50
2004-2005	1.35	190.39	0.70

Source: Office of the Central Excise and Land Custom, Government of India, Agartala.

Table 9.4: Status of Trade between Bangladesh and Tripura/NEI

Year	*Total value of Trade between Tripura and Bangladesh (Rs. In crores)*	*Total value of Trade Between NEI and Bangladesh (Rs. In crores)*	*Share of Tripura in Total value of Trade Between NEI and Bangladesh (in %)*
1999-2000	9.18	179.25	5.12
2000-2001	6.81	158.42	4.29
2001-2002	5.51	191.41	2.87
2002-2003	6.79	208.80	3.25
2003-2004	11.38	249.63	4.55
2004-2005	N.A	209.97	N.A

Source: Office of the Central Excise and Land Custom, Government of India, Agartala.

2003-2004 and 190.39 crores in 2004-2005. The percentage of Tripura's share in total exports of NEI is negligible.

The total value of trade during the period 1999-2000 and 2004-2005 is also found from Table- 9.4.It reveals that the Tripura's trade with Bangladesh has declined from Rs. 9.18 crores in 1999-2000 to Rs. 5.65 crores in 2001-02 but increased to Rs. 7.04 crores in 2002-03 and Rs. 11.56 crores in 2003-04. The total value of trade between NEI and Bangladesh, on the other hand, has increased from Rs. 179.25 crores in 1999-2000 to Rs. 251.53 crores in 2003-2004. The share of Tripura in total value of trade between NEI and Bangladesh in the year 2003-04 was only 4.59 per cent.

Hence it is quite clear that though there is an immense potentiality, the Indo-Bangla trade has really not developed through Tripura. Out of the seven Land Custom Stations– Agartala, Srimantapur, Muhurighat, Khowai, Dhalaighat, Manughat, Ragnabazar, only three stations i.e., Agartala, Srimantapur, Muhurighat are functional as far as formal trade transactions are concerned. NEI's share of imports are not quite large but regarding exports the States sharing borders with Bangladesh seem to enjoy a upper hand. The large reserves of minerals, production of horticultural products and a congenial trade atmosphere through border routes seem to help bilateral trade. Limestone and coal of NEI are exported to Bangladesh; hence the balance of trade is in favour of the North East with its value of exports much higher than the imports over the same period of time

Trade between India and Bangladesh have grown in the past 2 to 3 decades unprecedently. The major items of trade between Bangladesh and NEI are coal, limestone, fruits, ginger, boulder stone, marble stone, paper, auto parts, bamboo, betel leaf etc. (exports to Bangladesh) and fish, molasses, dry fish, jute, tiles, cotton waste, juice, mineral water, snacks and bakery items etc. (imports from Bangladesh). The items of import from Bangladesh to Tripura are fruit juices, potato crackers, mineral water, soaps, cashew–nut, mustard oil, soyabean oil, PVC pipes and tubes, synthetic fiber, stone chips etc. which seem to help the small and medium enterprises actively. Tripura exported ginger, betel leaves, fresh fruits, chilies, playing cards, natural rubber etc. Perhaps a lack of industrial infrastructure and a backward economy of the State may account for the fact that imports have remained constantly higher than exports in Tripura. Tripura is Bangladesh's gateway to the NEI. The nearest rail station on Bangladesh side from Agartala is Akhaura (8 km from Agartala, 125 km from Chittagang port).

Potential Areas of Trade

Bangladesh's comparative advantage in serving the northeast market with an estimated turnover of Rs.20,000 crore per annum is a potential market for developing trade relation from Bangladesh's perspective. It has been found that Bangladesh's exports to Tripura are much higher than the imports by Tripura in comparison to rest of northeast States. Hence, Bangladesh can explore the market of Tripura and even Tripura can do the same. The followings are the potential areas in which trade between Tripura and Bangladesh can be improved.

Tripura lags behind in economic development due to her poor infrastructural facilities. However, Tripura has immense reserves of gas which can generate power so essential for industrial , agricultural and commercial development. The State is endowed with natural gas reserves of 588 billion cu. m. which has huge potentiality to generate power in excess of Tripura's requirement. Recently the North Eastern Electric Power Corporation (NEEPCO) and other organizations have initiated setting up of gas based power projects with 500 MW capacity .If the target is achieved, Tripura will have a surplus in power generation. In the absence of any industrial base in the State Tripura can easily export the excess power to Bangladesh and neighbouring regions.

The agro-climatic Conditions

The agro-climatic conditions in Tripura are suitable for development of tea plantation. The soils are generally fertile, without any major problems of toxicity or deficiency. The average annual rainfall is about 2100 mm, with a fairly even distribution over the year. Tripura has a history of tea plantations going back to 1916. In fact, Tripura is categorized as a traditional tea-growing State – with about 60 tea estates and 3,000 small tea growers, producing about 7.5 million kg of tea every year. This makes Tripura the 5th largest, among the 14 tea producing States, after Assam, West Bengal, Tamil Nadu and Kerala. There is a considerable scope to increase the area under tea plantation as well as productivity. The tea currently produced in Tripura is recognized for its good blending qualities. Some plantations in the State are going for organic production of tea. There is considerable scope for the entrepreneurs of Bangladesh and Tripura. Tea produced in the State is at present sent to Guwahati or Calcutta for marketing. These can easily be marketed through Bangladesh.

Natural Rubber Production

In natural rubber production, Tripura ranks second only to Kerala in the country. More and more plantations are reaching yielding stage and the productivity levels are also encouraging. In view of the area under plantations together with the growth potential and rubber production trends, the State has been identified as the second rubber capital of the country. There is a vast potential for setting up of rubber-based industries in the State. The rubber produced in the State is also of high quality which faces trading problems in the absence of any rubber based industry in the State. In 2002-03 an area of about 17,701 hectare land was under natural rubber plantation in the State. Total rubber production was 17,849 MT and total value of rubber production was Rs. 69.42 crores in 2002-03 . The raw rubber now produced is being sent out to the neighbouring States for further value addition. Internal trade in India takes a long route through the narrow corridor in Assam which is both time consuming as well as expensive. If exported to Bangladesh or to other countries through Bangladesh port it will easily reduce the related expenses as well as ensure foreign exchange considerably.

Fruit Processing

Fruit processing is another potential area wherein bilateral trade between the two regions may be embarked upon. The agro-climatic conditions are favourable for growing various fruit and horticultural crops. The products of Tripura are well known-both in raw as well as processed form. There is scope for expansion of area under any specific variety, if required. A modern Food Processing Technology Park is being set up near Agartala, to give a fillip to this sector. An Agri Export Zone for pineapple is also being developed. There is a vast potential for setting up of food processing units in the State. Seasonal fruits such as pineapples, jackfruits, oranges, litchis etc. are grown in large quantities. These can be exported to Bangladesh for value addition. At present large quantities of these are informally traded with Bangladesh from Tripura. Other food products e.g. cashew nuts, vegetables and spices like pepper etc. too are commercially grown in Tripura . These products may be exported to Bangladesh instead of sending them to mainland India and facing the ensuing problems. Tripura can explore the market of Bangladesh in this regard.

Cane and Bamboo Handicraft

Tripura cane and bamboo handicrafts are considered to be among the best in the country for the exquisite designs, wide range of products and artistic appeal. This industry has a great export potential as well. Steps have been taken to develop this industry on modern lines. Not only that, in view of availability of large bamboo resources in the State, industrial products like bamboo tiles, laminated products, ply, boards, corrugated sheets etc. can be produced, which can be used as building materials, for furniture manufacture etc. Studies have shown that Bamboo is a very effective substitute for timber and is, in fact, better in many respects.

Tourism and Fauna & Flora

Tourism is perhaps one of the most vibrant areas of economic development of the present times. Tourism can build transnational communities as people can interact with each other and develop a deeper sense of appreciation, cooperation and ultimately remove all narrow barriers and create new potential friendship between the two countries. Tripura is an attractive tourist destination. The State has a rich cultural heritage. The State also has rich flora and fauna. There is also great potential for development of tourist circuits, involving all the NE States and if possible, Bangladesh as well. All this offers attractive opportunities for the Hospitality Industry. Tripura and Bangladesh have always shared a special bond culturally, linguistically, ethnically since the princely regime. Partition has cut across the land and separated families as well as blurred the memories of the old days. Bilateral cooperation may be boosted if tourism is given special attention nowadays. This will be possible if owing to geographical proximity people on the either side be allowed to cross over freely. An attempt to relax visa rules, substituting passport entry by permit rules, encouraging package tours and allowing private tour operators on both sides will perhaps lead to open border system. Reuniting families, creating a sense of oneness, preserving heritage monuments will lead to another segment of border trade, which will undoubtedly lead to increased revenue.

Transhipment Facility

Transit route through Bangladesh is one of the important areas for cooperation between two regions from Tripura's perspective. Due to its peculiar geographical location, the State is like an island and people of the State want a corridor to reach the mainland, which will be less expensive as well as less time taking. Recently Agartala-Kolkata via Dhaka bus service was launched and is running with high hopes. If transhipment facility through Bangladesh is allowed, it would be beneficial for both the regions. According to an estimate by the Tripura Chamber of Commerce, every day more than 1,000 trucks could be utilized for transhipment of Indian goods and Bangladesh can earn about Rs.2,000 crores per annum and Tripura can become the gateway to NEI.

Higher Education

The higher education that used to be considered as a public good is now increasingly being viewed as a private good. The efforts made by WTO legislating higher education as a private good, if implemented , then higher educational service would be treated like all other commodities and can be traded without much restriction. The higher education system in Tripura has deepened and widened over the period. Some significant changes have also taken place in higher education sector of the State in tune with new economic policies. Privatization has already started shaping higher education system in Tripura. One university and two technology and science colleges have been established in the private sector. A few more private universities and medical colleges are in the pipeline. .In view of above the State can explore the opportunity of providing higher education service to the students of Bangladesh. At present very few students from the adjacent area of Bangladesh come to Agartala for higher education observing all visa formalities. The computer related programmes are much sought after by the learners of Bangladesh.

Health Facilities

Health care is another area where Tripura can explore the opportunity to provide service to Bangladesh. At present there are a number of beds in all the hospitals of Tripura including private nursing homes. It is a widely known fact that 20-30 per cent of indoor and outdoor patients of hospitals and private nursing homes in Tripura are residents of Bangladesh . Most of them come illegally to this side of the border for better treatment. Relaxing Visa rules or introducing permit system or even simply allowing them for a few hours to consult doctors can legalize this service. People on both the sides of the border will be much benefited if this could be done.

Impediments

Trade Relations between Tripura and Bangladesh

A major barrier to develop the trade between Tripura and Bangladesh is lack of adequate infrastructure in both the regions. Among the major infrastructural constraints on Tripura's side which impede the development of trade are inadequate rail and road transport network in the State, poor road conditions, lack of cargo handling facilities, inadequate banking facilities as well as poor telecommunications, postal services etc.

It has been seen that of the seven land custom stations only three stations are functional for formal trade, i.e. Agartala, Srimantapur and Muhurighat. Even these stations lack in the basic amenities so necessary for carrying out brisk trade. First of all there are no warehousing facilities and since a major share of trade items are in perishable goods there is no scope of preserving them. Secondly there is no proper parking bay for trucks. Thirdly banking facilities exclusively to promote border-trade are almost non-existent. Fourthly, the documentation process in the custom stations is lengthy and even cumbersome which fails to attract traders to carry out trading formally. Fifthly, the stations lack in adequate staff strength too. Sixthly, it was seen that these stations lacked basic civic amenities so essential to carry out trading. Finally, there are no sales counters, shops, retailers near the custom stations, which can cater to these traders if and when required.

Transportation Facility

Transportation bottleneck is one of the most important problem of trade in Tripura's context. Tripura is linked with mainland by a narrow corridor which passes through Assam. Thus, goods, cargo transports from Delhi/Kolkata have to take a much longer route and involves more cost to reach the State. For example, it takes 3-4 days for the goods to reach Agartala from Kolkata. This increases the total cost of the traders at Agartala, the prices of essentials shoot up , even goods disappear from markets due to hoarding by unscrupulous traders and all these becomes more problematic when the roads are blocked due to landslides. The closed border, visa-permit regulations deter the two governments from allowing cargo/passengers through Bangladesh. Recently, a positive sign in this sphere was noticed when the over-land transit was allowed for passengers traveling to Kolkata from Agartala via Bangladesh. Though there are certain hurdles as the passengers have to be off-boarded in the border check posts and also have to change buses in Dhaka and at Benapole due to custom regulation and the timings of the bus services. However, the goods/cargo permit is still not initiated.

Communication System

The communication system of the State is very poor .It requires upgradation. The communication system comprises of postal service, telegraph service, telephone service, internet service etc. Communication facilities in the State have been growing slowly. Insurgency problem in the State is one of the main reasons for such slow development. The postal and telecommunication facilities should be expanded to the remotest area of the State so that border trade gets an impetus.

Informal Trade

One of the major impediments, which obstruct the free trade between Tripura and Bangladesh is the thriving informal trade. It perhaps requires no mention that there is considerable occurrence of informal trade between India and Bangladesh. This is the result of trade restrictions on the free flow of goods between the two countries .The value of informal exports to Bangladesh is reportedly in the range of US $350 to US $500 million every year (India Bangladesh Infrastructure Summit, 2000 Calcutta). Informal trade between NEI and Bangladesh is estimated at US $ 36 million in the year 2002 (Northeast India Bangladesh Initiative Map, 2004, BEI, Dhaka). Large volumes of trade between Tripura and Bangladesh continue, as the costs of trading in the informal channel are significantly lower than the formal channel. Earlier studies reveal that such traders have developed efficient mechanism for contract enforcement, information flows etc. The volume of informal trade cannot be ascertained in the value of foods seized but certainly the figures are astounding. The value of goods seized from Indo-Bangla border in Tripura is Rs.2.94 crores in 2003-04 and Rs. 4.35 crores in 2002-03 respectively.

Weekly Markets

There are also weekly markets operating in the border areas where agricultural products, household articles, bare necessities are sold to those living in close proximity. The value of such rules are never ascertained .

India had enjoyed a rail transit through erstwhile East Pakistan till 1965 but this was stopped after the Indo-Pak war. The nearest rail station of Tripura is on the Bangladesh side-Akhaura which is only 8 km from Agartala and 125 km from the Chittagong port. The snapping of rail route has affected the economy of Tripura and also encouraged informal trade. Though there is an agreement on Inland Water Transit and Trade, 1972 it was renewed in 22nd August 1995 effective from 4th October 1995 for a period of 2 years only. Under the protocol 8 river routes here been identified for cargo transit purposes but there no points on the river route touching Tripura. Surface transport is also bottleneck as cargo facilities are not initiated through the borders. Also there are no warehousing facilities available at border entry points on either side.

Another impediment was noticed that the traders/ entrepreneurs of Tripura were quite ignorant about the rules, regulations, documentation processes of border trade. It was found that these traders lacked in the aptitude towards export enterprise through proper channels.

Corruption and bribery among the government officials in connection with procurement of passport and visa, customs and excise clearance for border trade etc. is another important impediment in developing trade between the two regions.

Corruption in all these departments have been institutionalized to a noticeable extent. Without bribery it is simply impossible to get the work done in due time .

Strategies for Improvement

A strong trade axis between India and Bangladesh can surely build up cordial relations between the countries. India needs to come forward to boost economic relations. One of the ways could be removal of tariff barriers, which would promote greater trade as well as improve transportation facilities. Perhaps the two nations can also take a common stand together and uphold their mutual cooperation internationally. Tripura which shares an extensive border with Bangladesh can play a remarkably significant role.

Various study groups and experts have identified the impediments in Tripura for developing trade with Bangladesh. The strategy should therefore be framed to remove all such impediments for making a climate conducive for development of border trade with Bangladesh. It is to be remembered that the task of fencing the Indo-Bangla border in Tripura will be completed very soon. It is expected that the informal trade between the two regions will decrease significantly. On the other hand formal trade will grow at a faster rate. Any attempt to develop border trade be viewed at a wider perspective involving Tripura Chamber of Commerce, TIDC, banks and financial institutions, export promotion council , customs department etc.

Moreover the Strategy should aim for the following:

i. Development of infrastructure at land custom stations. Modernizing and upgrading of infrastructure of LCSs also calls for immediate attention.

ii. Making more land custom stations of the State functional for border trade.

iii. Banking facilities are to be extended to all LCSs.

iv. Negotiations with Bangladesh through central government for goods transit from West Bengal to Tripura.

v. Proposal for establishing railway link between Agartala and Akhaura in Bangladesh.

vi. Taking initiative for joint venture in the areas of rubber, fruit processing, tea and gas based power sector.

vii. Textile industry is quite developed in Bangladesh specially readymade garments production. India has a strong primary textile industry with ample raw material supply. If the two countries make an alliance in this sector it will provide a win-win situation and even allow them to become globally competitive. Tripura may join in if an office operates from here.

viii. Encouraging the travel operators for package tours in both the regions to boost tourism.

ix. Establishing the office of export promotion council.

x. Motivating entrepreneurs of the State for establishing border trade related venture through seminar, workshop and entrepreneurship training programme.

xi. Export route may be extended via waterway. Tripura's south district is barely 15 km away from the Bay of Bengal through Feni river. Though there is yet no canal or sluiced gate as an outlet to the sea, attempt may be taken to avail of waterways through Chittagong to Paradeep or even further down West Coast.

xii. Roads, riverine tracts to be improved .

xiii. Cargo gate for entry/exit to be separated from the passenger gates.

xiv. Simplification and standardization of documentation facilities to avoid procedural impediments at borders, also lesser disparity in rail freights.

xv. Open border–transit system can made Tripura the Gateway to NE and India.

This could even legalize informal trade.

xvi. Give Bangladeshi goods free access to Indian Market.

Conclusion

Tripura had been a strategically important trading centre for undivided Bengal's wares in the past. Undoubtedly Partition has acted as a rigid barrier between the two regions, yet it is now a settled fact in cross border relations .However trade between the two can once again bring together the severed kinship ties reviving the memories of the good old days as well as the region may act as a go-between corridor in the South East Asian and European Community Trade.

The location of Tripura is strategic in the International context, situated between Bangladesh on one side and south East Asia on the other. In the past, the State had natural communication links–roads, rail and waterways – with and through Bangladesh. Efforts are on for revival of these. Many major cities of Bangladesh and towns in Tripura are closely located, such as Agartala –Dhaka –150 km; Kailashahar-Sylhet–90 km, Sabroom–Chittagong-75 km, Sonamura–Comilla-25 km. etc. The direct distance between Agartala and Kolkata, through Bangladesh, is only 350 km.

While the volume of unofficial trade as assessed by an IIFT study exceeds Rs.100 crores (1997-98), official trade has grown four-fold since 1995-96. There is great scope for this to grow further. The declared goal of a free trade area and trends of reduction of tariff and non-tariff barriers make the integration of the region's economy with adjoining parts of Bangladesh foreseeable in near future. Serious and conscious efforts are to be taken to develop linkages with industry and commerce organizations of Bangladesh to expand economic ties for mutual benefit. The State has to gear up to perform its natural and geographically assigned role of the Gateway to the North East India.

REFERENCES

Bangladesh-India Chamber of Commerce and Industries (2000): *India Bangladesh Infrastructure Summit,* December 21, 2000, Calcutta. (www. saarcnet. com/ newsaarcnet /publications/summit.html)

Bhattacharya, Jayanta (2001): *Tripura–Bangla: From History to Future,* paper presented at the third dialogue on interaction with Indian Bordering States, organized by the Bangladesh Institute of International and Strategic Studies, Dhaka, August 21-23, 2001.

Bhattacharya, Pallab: *Indo-Bangla Trade, PTI Feature.* (www. sentinelassam.com/sentinel_en/archives/aug1704/editorial.htm)

Chakraborty, Kiran Sankar and Das, B.C. (2002): An inside into the development of SSI in Tripura, *Southern Economist,* 41, (8), Bangalore.

Dahiya, L.N. (2004): India's International Trade in Higher Education, *Indian Journal of Commerce,* 57, (3).

Das, Gangadhar(2004):fruits and Vegetables Production in North Eastern Region: Export potential, *The Indian Journal of Commerce,* 57, (3).

Das, B.C. (2004): Health Care Facilities in Tripura, paper presented in the national seminar organized by the Department of Economics, Tripura University and ESSOT, Agartala on 18th – 19th September 2004 at Agartala.

Government of Tripura (2000): Speech of Minister, Industries and Commerce, Government of Tripura in 'First National Conference of Small Scale Industries,' Vigyan Bhavan, New Delhi 30th August, 2000.

Government of Tripura, Department of Industries and Commerce (2004): *Tripura The Land of Opportunities,* Agartala.

Government of Tripura, Department of Industries and Commerce (2002): Speech of Chief Minister, Tripura, in the seminar on 'Promotion of Trade and Investment Between Tripura and Bangladesh', 31st May 2002.

Government of Tripura, Department of Industries and Commerce and Tripura Chamber of Commerce (2002): Proceedings of seminar on 'Promotion of Trade and Investment Between Tripura and Bangladesh', 31st May 2002

Jalil Altaf (2004): Northeast India-Bangladesh Initiatives Map, Bangladesh Enterprise Institute, Dhaka.

Verghese, B.G. (2002): Tripura eyes Bangladesh, *The Statesman*, 22th June 2002.

10

Forest Rights Act: Implications of *Jhumias* of Tripura

It is a universally accepted proposition today that the right of the tribal shifting cultivators of Tripura is related to the forests and policies followed by the Government. The objective of the paper is to assess the impact of Schedule Tribes and Traditional Forest Dwellers (Recognition of Forest Rights) Act, 2006 notified on 1st January 2008 on the jhumias of Tripura.

The tribal population of Tripura is around 31 per cent of the total Tribal population according to 2001 Census. It is possible to divide the Tribal population of Tripura into three categories for policy purposes. The first category consists of Tribals who are indigenous to the State, they are Tripuris, Reangs, Jamatias, Noatias, Koloi, Rupini, and Murasing. In the second category are the tribes who have a major presence in the neighbouring States of Tripura, they are Lushai, Kuri, Halam, Mogs and Chakmas. Also, Garo, Khasis, Lepchas and Bhutias fall in this category. In the third category belong the tribes who have come from main land India, they are: Munda, Santan, Orang and Bhils. It should be noted that the Reangs are classified as "Primitive Tribal group." A large number of Reangs are wholly dependent on Jhum cultivation. This classification of tribes is helpful in two ways.

First, it indicates the difference among the tribes of Tripura in terms of their socio-economic development. The that have been identified to be the most primitive. Reangs are involved in shifting cultivation in a great number. This is not true for the tribes in the third category like the Bhils. Bhils were brought to Tripura mainly for working as labourers in tea plantations. This diversity in occupational pattern is highlighted by the threefold classification of the tribes made in the present paper.

Second, the threefold classification highlights the importance of community specific development programmes. There can be no universal approach to tribal development in the context of Tripura.

Tribal Life and Culture

Interface of Forests and Tribal life and culture in Tripura has a long history going back to time immemorial. Tribal communities in Tripura had practiced *'jhum'* cultivation, which is based on clearing a forest area in a particular season. The community shifted from this plot of cultivated land to return to the same plot after many years. The numbers of years it took to come back to the same area for cultivation is often called a 'jhum cycle'. When total population of the *'jhumias'*, i.e., the shifting cultivators was small and the track of forests they would roam around was relatively vast, the *'jhum* cycle' was long of around 15 to 20 years. Since productivity of jhum cultivation depends on the quality of forests burned down to prepare the land for cultivators so if the period is long *'jhum* cycles' the productivity of *'jhum'* land was quite high. This helped the *jhum* based tribal economy not only to meet their needs for food but provided them a surplus which they could trade with the plains people to purchase good they could not produce like salt, dry fish and edible oil. In this manner the *jhum* based tribal economy sustained itself for thousands of years. Since *jhum* cultivation is a multi-crop cultivation system, so the *jhum* economy did not only produce paddy but also vegetables, mustard oil seeds, jute etc. The non-food crops had been traded in considerable quantity in the period of long *jhum* cycles. However, all tribal people of Tripura were not *'jhumias'*. One can broadly identify two types of tribal communities is Tripura. One type is the *jhum* based tribals (Tripuris, Jamatias and Reangs) who practice it even now. The other type had been brought to Tripura mainly in the plantations, especially tea plantations, from the mainland. Their socio-economic condition differs significantly from that of the *jhumia*. However, the practice of shifting cultivation became less became productive as *jhum* cycles got shorter. This was due to population increase on the one hand. But equally important was the introduction of Forests Acts of the government which legally denied access to forests for the tribal communities in the 'Reserved Forests'.

The outcome of growing population to feed on the one hand and shortage of *jhum* land on the other hand was shortening of the '*jhum* cycles'. *Jhum* cycles began to get shorter and shorter in Tripura and fell from 15 to 20 years cycles to 1 to 3 years cycles. These had two important consequences, one, falling productivity of *jhum* because the land lacked in nutrients due to shorter cycles. The other is the degradation of the forests as frequent *jhumming* did not allow natural growth of forests which the earlier larger cycles could ensure.

Schemes for resettlement of *Jhumias*

The lower productivity meant lower living standard for the *jhumias*. They became the poorest of the poor of the State, their health deteriorated due to lack of food, the children suffered from malnutrition. The plight of the jhumias can only be seen to be believed.

There are various schemes to resettle the *jhumias* of Tripura which were initiated from early 1950s. However, the number of *jhumia* households in Tripura is still quite considerable. The Department of Agriculture of Government of Tripura estimated from 2001 census that the number of jhumias in 2001 was 297000. Unfortunately various government departments have different figures. According to DFO, Forests Department of the government of Tripura, the jhumia population is estimated to be 102,269 for Dhalai District alone in the year 2006. The number of *jhumia* families was 20664 in Dhalai. If it is assumed that each *jhumia* family cultivates on the average one hectare land than more than 20,000 hectare or about 10% of reserved forest area of the District is affected by jhum cultivation per year. In the case of North Tripura District , the area affected is around 28 per cent of the forests land. This assumes around 33000 *jhumias* in North Tripura District. This indicates the environmental consequences of jhum cultivation in the period of shortened *Jhum* Cycles.

History of Forest Acts

Before discussing the major features of Forest Rights Acts, 2006, one may look at the historical aspects of forests acts in Tripura very briefly.

Indian Forest Act of 1927 was adopted by the Government of India in 1947. It remains the basic Act for forests management in India. When Tripura merged with the Indian Union in 1949 the Act became effective for the State also. Tripura attained statehood in 1972. The government of Tripura has notified various rules under this Act. The 1927 Act (Chapter II-1o) was not totally oblivious to the needs of the shifting cultivations and recognized the need for granting them certain land for settlement. However, in most cases the claims of the shifting cultivations were rarely given a legal recognition. Therefore, often the tribals continued to practice *jhum* even within reserved forests without any legal basis.

It is in this context that one can study the major features of Forest Rights Act of 2006. The major features of the Act can be summarized as follows:

1. The Act recognises and vests forest rights and occupation in forest land in forest dwelling scheduled tribes and other international forest dwellers who have been residing in the forest area for three generations(75years) prior to 13-12-2005, i.e. from 13-12-1930.

2. The Act provides for the ceiling of occupation of forest land on the basis of the area under actual occupation and in no case exceeding an area of four hectare.

3. The Act recognises the right of 'ownership access' to collect use and dispose of minor forest produce. Minor forest produce shall include non-timber forest produce of plant origin including.
   a) bamboo
   b) brush wood
   c) stumps
   d) cane
   e) tussar
   f) cocoons
   g) honey
   h) wax
   i) lac
   j) kendu leaves
   k) medicinal plants
   l) herbs, roots and tubers,etc.
4. The Act recognises the right to in situ (i.e. original area) rehabilitation including alternative land in cases of illegal eviction or displacement without legal entitlement to rehabilitation prior to 13.12.2005.
5. The Act permits the government to divert forest land for the purpose schools, hospitals, anganwadis, roads, drinking water supply etc.
6. As per the Act, the gram sabha has been designated as the competent authority for initiating the process of determining the nature and extent of individual or community forest rights.

In a letter to the chief ministers, the Prime Minister of India had called the Act as piece of *"landmark legislation."* The introduction of the final Act had been through strong opposition from paper and pulp companies, forest bureaucracy and 'conservation fundamentalist.' The Act proposes to correct the historical injustice meted out to the forest dwelling tribals. The Act also asserts that the rights so obtained go with the duties of sustainable use of forests and conservation of bio-diversity.

Approach to Tribal Development

Recognising the rights of the forest-dwellers, allowing for their settlement in forest areas, providing school, health and other facilities like drinking water and electricity shall no doubt go a long way in improving the living standard of the forest-dwelling jhumias of Tripura. This process can be made more sustainable if education and skill brings about occupational diversification among them to remove the problem of over-dependence on land based resources. With expanding population, per capita availability of land is bound to decline for land-based people. This long-term perspective has to be taken in assessing the implications of Forest Right Act.

REFERENCES

Deb Burman S.B.K. *A study over the Jhum and Jhumia Rehabilitation in the Union Territory of Tripura,* Government of Tripura, Agartala, 1971.

Ramkrishnan, Venkitesh (2008): *Hope and Fear, Frontline,* Feb 29, 2008.

11

Management of Higher Education Institutions in Tripura

A TQM Approach

Higher education conventionally refers to the studies beyond school level, universities, colleges and other institutions of higher learning are its main establishments. Despite the increase in numbers, the performance of these establishments is not always upto the expectation. The quality of higher education in the State has become questionable primarily because of inadequate responsiveness to changing environment created by factors like information explosion and globalisation. Along with this, financially unsustainable increase in enrolment for higher studies make it imperative for most of the institutions in Tripura to ensure the relevance and quality of their programmes as well as products. In this backdrop, an attempt has been made in this article as to how the concept of Total Quality Management (TQM), can be extended to the higher education institutions of Tripura.

State of Higher Education Institutions

One of the basic features of higher education in Tripura is that the entire domain is under the State government. However, a private university and a private Science College have been established recently. The first higher education institution of the State, Maharaja Bir Bikram College, was set up in 1947. After the merger of the princely State of Tripura with the Union of India there has been a marked increase in the number of such establishments. At present in the field of higher education, excluding the above mentioned private establishments, there is an University, 14 general degree colleges and seven professional and technical Colleges. These institutions are catering to the need of more than 19,000 students with 439 full time and nearly 500 part-time faculty members.

Despite the increase in number, the performance of many of these institutions is not always satisfactory resulting in poor academic quality. Truly speaking, shortage of funds, inadequate infrastructure, improper planning, insufficient teaching staff and above all unsustainable increase in enrolment for higher studies make it impossible for most of the institutions to ensure the quality of their programmes. It is evident

From Table 11.1 that there are a few general degree colleges where the number of enrolled students is very meager. It is quite a matter of concern, both socially and economically, how far this is justified. For example, Government Degree College, Amarpur has 138 students or Ambedkar College has 119 students. On the other hand Maharaja Bir Bikram College has 3487 students or Women's College has 2821 students.

Quality in Education

It is very difficult to define quality in education for several reasons. Like justice or freedom, quality in education can be experienced but cannot be defined. Instead, it would be appropriate to consider few characteristics or variables, which are relevant for de terming the quality like teacher-student ratio, infrastructural facilities, facilities for extra-curricular activities and dedication of the teachers. Besides the above, other related or auxiliary varieties may also be considered if necessary. For instance, along with the size of the teaching staff, an index of their qualifications or along with the size of the students, their academic performance at entry level may also be considered.

The quality of higher education is thus, closely associated with the above variables, few of which cannot be measured

Table 11.1: Higher Education Establishment in Tripura as on 31-03-2003 (General Degree College)

Name of College	*Students Enrolment*	*No. of Subjects Offered**	*Full time Teachers*	*No. of students per teacher***	*No. of teacher per subject*	*Pass out rate*
Ambedkar College	119	07	03	40	0.43	45%
Belonia College	2361	29	30	79	1.03	34%
B.B.M. College	814	18	24	34	1.33	22%
D.D.M College	1065	17	17	63	1.00	46%
Govt. DegreeCollege, Amarpur	138	06	05	28	0.83	43%
Govt. Degree College, Dharmanagar	1139	17	16	71	0.94	23%
Govt. DegreeCollege, Kamalpur	259	10	04	65	0.40	NA
M.M.D. College, Sabroom	169	06	05	34	0.83	29%
K.N.Mahavidyalaya	450	07	06	75	0.8q,	23%
MBB College	3487	37	82	43	2.22	38%
N.S.Mahavidyalaya	1417	17	20	71	1.18	NA
R.K.Mahavidyalaya	1083	18	16	68	0.89	43%
R.T.Coliege	2094	22	35	60	1.59	23%
Women's College	2821	28	57	50	2.03	NA
All the Collegestaken together(Grand Total)	17,416	239	320	54	1.34	32%

* Ignored part time teachers.

** Ratio between number of students initially admitted in last year and the students passout final examination.

Table 11.2: Higher Education Establishments in Tripura as on 31-03-2003 (professional & Technical Colleges and University)

Name of Establishment	*Student Enrolment*	*No. of Fulltime teachers*	*Course offered*	*No. of student per teachers**	*Academic Performance.**
IASE	121	12	B.Ed M.Ed. CTE	10	Satisfactory
Govt. of Art &Craft	218	02	BV A (Hons.)	109	Satisfactory
Govt. MusicCollege	54	10	R Muse.	05	Satisfactory
RegionalInstitute ofPharmaceutical Science andTechnology	25	07	B. Pharma D. Pharma	04	Satisfactory
RegionalCollege ofPhysicalEducation	21	05	RP.Ed.	04	Satisfactory
TripuraEngineering College	625	30	RE.	21	Satisfactory
Tripura Govt.Law College	143	02	LL.B (Hons.)	71	Satisfactory
Tripura University	959	51	MasterDegree -12	19 Nos.	Satisfactory
All the Establishment Taken together (Grand Total)	2166	119		18	Satisfactory

Source: Annual Reports, 2001-2002 & 2002-2003, Tripura University

* Ignored Part-time teachers

easily. However, the institutions of higher studies are usually rated on the basis of their performance related to certain prescribed parameters.

National Assessment and Accreditation Council (NAAC) has identified the following seven criteria to serve as the basis of its assessment producers:

(i) Curricular aspects,
(ii) Teaching-learning and evaluation,
(iii) Research, consultancy and extension,
(iv) Infrastructure and learning resources,
(v) Student support and progression,
(vi) Organisation and Management, and
(vii) Healthy practices.

Understanding variance in the type of institutions, the seven criteria have been allotted differential weightages for Universities, Autonomous Colleges and Affiliated Colleges (Table 11.3).

Table 11.3: Parameters and respective weightages for Assessing Educational Institutions (NAAC)

Parameter	*Universities*	*Autonomous Colleges*	*Affiliated Colleges*
Teaching-learning and Evaluation	25	30	40
Curriculum Aspects	15	15	10
Research, Consultancy and Extension	15	10	05
Student Support and Progression	15	15	15
Infrastructure and Learning Resources	10	10	10
Organisation and Management	10	10	10
Healthy Practices	10	10	10
Total	100	100	100

Steps to develop TQM in the Institutions of Higher Studies

Higher education in Tripura, is such an area where despite huge investment by government, society's requirement, perhaps, has not been met. In view of the social needs and globalisation of opportunities TQM in the higher education Institutions of Tripura is justified. Moreover it reduces wastage in education and increases its efficiency by pursuing the idea of maximization of the use of amenities provided for a given amount of expenditure, or, alternatively the minimization of the amount of expenditure required for providing a given set of facilities.

While applying TQM in the institutions of higher studies of Tripura following are the necessary steps required to develop the concept subject to modification or alteration to suit individual institutions:

1. Awareness about quality in education to be developed among the authorities, management, teachers, students, guardians and employees of the institutions. Organising Seminars/Workshop in this regards might be helpful.

2. Set the goals of the institutions to achieve the desired quality.

3. Forget that there is no further scope of improvement in quality in the process of imparting education to students.

4. The system should aim at taking account of the development of joint responsibilities too.

5. Ensure that the responsibility of each teacher as individual or group (college-wise, faculty-wise or department-wise) is clearly specified.

6. Students are to be considered as 'output' of the institution and the teachers, on the other hand are the main 'architects'.

7. The parents and employers in particular, and society in general are the ultimate beneficiary of quality output.

8. Consider NAAC prescribed parameters to describe quality in education which will help in accreditation too.

9. Ascertain in the internal and external factors which hinder the quality improvement.

10. The achievement of quality in education may require higher levels of skill, knowledge and management. Therefore, a result oriented approach has to be developed, specially in dealing with recruitment, promotion and posting of teachers in the Government degree colleges.

11. Quality programme may also require additional finance, which are to be procured well in advance by tapping the possible sources. Enhancement of fees for higher studies in Tripura may be considered in this regard.

12. Review or introduce reward system so that it supports the objective of TQM, The system for students may include scholarships, exemption from paying fees, awarding certificates of honour or medals, etc. while the system for teacher may include financial as well as non-financial rewards like additional opportunities for further studies or research, promotion, etc. In this context, different kind of scholarship programme of the State government for higher studies may come under review.

13. Develop appropriate just-in-time (JIT) so that every thing goes on as per scheduled programmes and well designed academic calendar.

14. Measuring quality in education or appropriate system for laying down standards etc. are all good, but significant results from TQM will not be obtained unless total commitment to quality is achieved.

Conclusion

It may be stated that the quality of higher education cannot be improved unless financial inputs are increased in proportion to requirements in a planned way. It is worthwhile to mention here that costs per student for higher education is huge in comparison to primary and secondary education, and government expenditure per student is also high and rising rapidly. Social rates of return incorporating the external benefits reaped by the society as a whole is a matter of concern for all. Standardisation of higher education is, thus, much sought after.

TQM, however, calls for much more than just standardisation of education. Unless the quality of teaching and research is constantly improved, educational institutions in Tripura would become stagnant and consequently fall behind the other States to deliver quality education. Here TQM can playa crucial role as it imbibes the concept of perpetual need for quality improvement as against static standardized system and encompasses all the sections of the entire programme.

REFERENCES

Bonner (1992): Total Quality Education, *Public Administration Review,* September-October.

British Standards Institutions (1991): *Quality Vocabulary* Part-2, London.

Chakraborty, K.S. (1997): TQM Concept in Higher Education of India, *Vidyasagar University Journal of Commerce,* Vol.2, March.

Chakraborty, K.S. and Haldar, P.K. (1998) : Re-engineering Higher Education in India, Business Studies, Department of Commerce, Calcutta University, Vol. XXI, July.

Chaterjee, Achintya (1994): Quality Excellence or Extinction, *The Indian Journal of Commerce,* Vol. XVIII, Part-3, No. 180, Sept, pp. 52-54.

Chowdhury, N.R.(1996): Higher Education Delivery Systems- Trying the TQM Option, *University News,* Sep.

Crawford and Shutler (1999): Total Quality Management in Education, problems and issues for classroom teachers, *The International Journal of Educational Management.*

Crosby (1979): Quality is free: Art of Marking Quality Certain, McGraw-Hill,

Deming (1986): *Out of the Crisis,* Cambridge University Press.

Gilmore (1974): *Product Conformance Cost,* Quality Progress.

Government of Tripura, (2002) : Education Department, *Higher Education Scenario of Tripura.*

Hansen and Jackson (1996): *TQM in the classroom, Quality in Higher Education.*

Juran (1988): *Quality Control Handbook,* McGraw-Hill, New York.

Motwani and Lumar (1997) The need for implementing *TQM* in Education, *Intemation Joumal of Educational Management.*

National Assessment and Accreditation Council (2002): *NAAC A Profile,* Bangalore.

Mukhapadhyay (2000) *Management of Quality in Higher Education, University News.*

Oakland (1993): *TQM,* Oxford.

Sallis(1996): *TQM in Education,* London, Kogan Paul.

Subramanyam, K. (1996): 'Total Quality Management in Higher Studies', *The Hindu,* June, Madras, p. 26.

Sherr and Lozier (1991): *TQM in Higher Education,* San Francisco.

Tripura University: *Annual Report* (2002-2003).

12

Higher Education in Tripura : A Vision for 2020

Introduction

The presence of a large number of educated unemployed as revealed in employment exchange data in the North Eastern Region (NER) of India has drawn the attention of policy-makers at the national and regional levels. Massive educated unemployed are not only wastage of a very precious human resource but also can be at the root of a sense of alienation among the youths of the North Eastern Region of India.

The Conceptual Frame of Analysis

The problem of educated unemployed can be best analysed using the standard demand-supply model. Educated unemployment is an indicator of a mismatch between demand and supply. On the demand side, primary sector including agriculture, forestry, mining and quarrying, pisci-culture and so on is likely to generate demand for educated and skilled labour as better technology and management are employed to modenize this sector. However, if there is stagnation in this sector then insufficient demand creates the possibility of unemployment in the skilled and educated labour force. Similar arguments apply for the manufacturing sector and the service sector. In other words, without a rapid growth of production in these sectors which can absorb the growing labour force, it will be difficult to reduce the problem of unemployment of educated youth of NER. On the supply side, the higher education system plays a vital role in determining the 'employability' of the young people coming out of the system. However, this is not to say that the only job of the colleges and universities is placement of the students for different jobs and occupations. Doing research in fundamental sciences may not directly lead to employment or may not bear fruit. Yet mankind's hunger for knowledge cannot be ignored by the institutions of higher education. However, greater emphasis must be placed on the employment generation aspect of higher education. In other words, it is the instrumental value of higher education rather than its intrinsic value which has to be given the highest priority in the resource constrained economy of NER of India.

SWOT Analysis of Higher Education System in Tripura

Before designing a perspective plan for education in Tripura on the basis of the principles of inclusive education on the one hand and employment generation or value addition of the labour force, on the other, it is necessary to carry out an analysis of the present situation of higher education in terms of its Strengths, Weaknesses, Opportunities and Threats. This may be presented as follows:

Strengths

1. The number of degree colleges has increased exponentially in last five to ten years in Tripura. This is a quantitative improvement which forms the basis of improvement in quality on the criteria of inclusive education on the one hand and employment generation on the other.

2. The participation of private initiative in degree colleges has increased in recent years indicating greater demand for college education of the people of Tripura.

3. There has been stagnation in the courses offered to the students in the past. However, in recent years new subjects and courses are being introduced with specific market orientation.

4. Before 1987, there was no university in the State of Tripura. Tripura University came into being due to the vision of political leadership. Tripura University has now turned into a Central University because it was hoped that this will help the university to grow both in terms of quality and quantity. Moreover, the State government encouraged private universities to join in the struggle for higher education in Tripura. As a result, there are two Universities in the State at present.

5. There has been an expansion in terms of professional and technical colleges also. Two medical colleges have been established. There is Tripura Institute of Technology in addition to the National Institute of Technology. There is a nursing college and a polytechnic college for female students. Therefore, the higher education scenario has diversified itself to a considerable extent in Tripura.

6. A greater emphasis is being placed on communication skills of the students which is essential for their employability. Spoken English courses are being introduced in the degree colleges.

7. Courses of Diploma and Bachelor in Computer Applications had been introduced in some of the degree colleges.

8. There is a concerted effort to improve the infrastructure of the degree colleges in terms of more spacious and modern class room and lecture halls, library buildings, computer facilities with internet connections, sports facilities, sanitation and drinking water.

Weaknesses

1. The availability of teachers with regular employment is insufficient in the case of most of the Degree Colleges in Tripura. Scarcity of teachers of English in the colleges is most acute.

2. The libraries are not well-equipped to meet the emerging requirements of teachers and students. IT enabled services

for the college libraries remain the greatest need of the hour. There is insufficient supply of journals in the libraries which provide the students and teachers with the most current developments in their study units. Inter-lending facilities between the college libraries do not exist. Photo copy facilities are not sufficient in the libraries. Modern management systems are not in place in the libraries.

3. The laboratories are not well-equipped in the case of science stream.

4. Public address systems for large class rooms are not available in the Colleges.

5. Inadequate number of class-rooms is also a major problem for most of the Colleges.

6. Many Colleges do not have proper boundaries and proper security system to discourage threat and misuse of class rooms.

7. Safe-drinking water facilities are not available in most of the Colleges.

8. Hygienic and cheap food catering services for students and teachers are not available in most of the Colleges.

9. Colleges do not have proper and clean premises and lavatories in some cases.

10. There is no medical check-up system and medical insurance system for the College students.

11. The colleges do not have dedicated electricity lines and as a result, teaching and laboratory work suffer when there are power fluctuations.

12. Very few colleges have replaced the traditional chalk-duster system by over head projectors and other advanced methods of class room presentation and interaction.

13. Well-equipped gymnasiums and playgrounds are conspicuous by their absence in most of the colleges.

14. A forestation and botanical gardens and other environmental concerns have not received their due attention in some of the Colleges of Tripura.
15. Sufficient furniture, like tables, almirahs etc. in a personalized space are not available for the teachers which hamper their academic and research activities.
16. Quarters in the college premises for teachers and other staff are not available in most of the Colleges.
17. Girls' hostels are not often properly provided or suitably utilized.
18. Study leave for research is not enjoyed by any of the College teachers though it is an important component of faculty development and improvement in the quality of teachers.

Opportunities

1. There is a strong opportunity of providing inclusive education in Tripura leading to an increase in the enrolment ratio of young people belonging to Scheduled Castes, Scheduled Tribes, Minorities and Other Backward Communities not only in Arts stream but also in professional, scientific and technical courses.
2. Since the initiative to create new infrastructure facilities is happening in a clean slate, therefore, one can plan creatively and bring modern facilities to the colleges of Tripura.
3. Similarly, there is a possibility of recruiting fresh minds with exposure to modern thinking and technology in the teaching profession.
4. Syllabus can be given a more modern stance and employment orientation since the new courses can be more easily accommodated by late comers in the education system which tradition bound systems find difficult to accept.

Threats

1. Financial sustainability of higher education in Tripura will not only require sustained budgetary support but also some cost sharing between the local community, Panchayati Raj Institutions, State Governments and the Central Government where an acceptable framework must give equal importance to equity and efficiency. However, without a rapid increase in production and productivity in the primary and secondary sectors of the economy, this effort at financial cost sharing will turn out to be difficult indeed. In fact, due to the fragmented nature of the economy of Tripura, a long-run term commitment of the Central Government remains a vital factor. Political instability in the Central Government and uncomfortable swings in perceptions about the North Eastern Region (NER) of India in general and Tripura in particular remains an area of concern for the people living in this region.

2. Civil society in this region looks at the relation between the Central Government and the State Government articulations in terms of political party based affiliations rather than common concerns for development of the State and the region. Coordinated action by the eight States of NER is also vitiated by political rather than a broader visionary movement representing the expectations and aspirations of the common people of this part of India. This narrow perspective hampers proper placement of demand on the Central Government and carrying out of responsibilities by the State Governments.

Suggestions

The suggestions for formulation of vision statement of higher education in Tripura for 2020 have to be placed in the context of the SWOT analysis presented above. Two essential matters must be borne in mind in the formulation of the vision statement.

First, it must be recognised that different States of India are at different stages of transition in higher education. These stages can be identified on the basis of four parameters. They are:

1. Creating access to the community in higher education. Indicators of access have to be properly formulated in any vision document. One indicator can be number of educational institutions per 10,000 population. Another indicator can be distance of the academic institutions from major habitations. The construction of proper indicators is an essential component of identifying the stage of transition.
2. Enrollment of students in higher education is another important indicator of transition. Gross enrolment ratio and net enrolment ratio on the basis of gender, caste and communities can help to identify the level of inclusiveness of higher education in a particular State or region.
3. Outcome indicators like transition rates and drop out rates provide the third aspect of the education process.
4. At the final stage, one can think about quality both in terms of employment of students and in terms of research outputs and contribution to national and international discourses in different spheres of knowledge.

The States of India in general and NER of India in particular can be mapped on the basis of these four parameters of higher education. One cannot deny that the NER States are at first stage of transition where access and enrolment are the major issues. Therefore, the vision statements must place the greatest emphasis on these two aspects.

Second, the vision can be broadly articulated as further strengthening of the strengths identified in the SWOT analysis and removing the weaknesses in a time profile of five years, ten years and fifteen years. As a final destination, the journey of higher education is an endless journey where the milestones keep on changing as we move from one stage to another.

13

Industrial Development Path of Less Developed Regions in the Era of Globalisation: Contours of a Roadmap for North-east India

Introduction

The current liberalised global regime has resulted in a massive relocation of industries across the globe. In the pre-globalisation era protectionist measures of the host country were the main pull factors, which are being replaced more and more by market forces. In the globalisation phase, efficiency consideration dominates investment decision of market players. Firms invest abroad for three reasons, namely, ownership specific advantages, internalization advantages and locational advantages. This in turn depends on the level of development of the host country. Relocation of industries does not necessarily mean the shifting of existing industries from one place to another due to easier transborder mobility created by globalisation. It also means grabbing of new opportunities created by globalisation due to its various kind of advantages. As a result of advantages in new destination, investment will flow towards new location instead of old location.

Globalisation is perhaps, one of the most debated issues in recent times throughout the world. Its impact in a developing country like India is immense. The term 'Globalisation' has different meaning to different stakeholders. It affects society at various levels and in its various dimensions–social, political, economic and cultural (Kumar, 2004). In its economic dimension it implies a process of transnationalisation of production and capital and standardisation of consumer tastes and their legitimization with the help of international bodies such as the World Bank, IMF and WTO. (Devadas, 2001). After independence India had introduced State control to facilitate economic development. Therefore, globalisation to India means a series of economic reforms towards liberalisation and privatization. This process in India began in 1991 unlike other countries where it started in the 1980s. After completion of first generation reforms our country is now passing through the second-generation reforms. First generation reforms were associated with industrial deregulation, opening the economy to trade, disinvestments and privatisation, financial sector reforms and private financing of infrastructure. The second generation reforms are characterized by extending reforms to the States, labour legislation, the functioning of the legal system, bringing duty structure at the global standard etc. (Ahuwalia, 2001).

Impact of globalisation is being experienced by most of the developing countries and India is no exception. India has reaped benefits of globalisation in terms of growth in GDP, inflow of FDI, forex reserve and technology transfers. However, it has also been observed that the opportunities created by globalisation have not reached all the regions of our country equally. This raises a serious concern for policy makers regarding the process of integration of industrially backward regions in the mainstream. An attempt has been made in this paper to analyse and understand the industrial development path of less developed regions like North-East Region of India.

Thus, the present paper aims to discuss the issues associated with industrial relocation in the era of globalisation with special reference to North-eastern Region of India. To be more specific the objectives of the chapter are i) to review the growth of Indian industry during globalisation regime. ii) to review the developmental approaches especially industrial development concerning North-east India iii) to propose a roadmap for growth of industry in North-east India to reap the opportunities of industrial relocation. and iv) to focus upon the potential areas for development of industry in North-eastern Region of India where industrial relocation can take place in future.

The chapter has six sections including the present one where the focal theme of the chapter is being introduced. Section two deals with the growth of Indian Industry during reforms era. Section three focuses upon the potential for development of industry in north-eastern region of India. Developmental approaches for North-east India and an alternative roadmap for growth of industry in North-eastern Region of India are discussed in the section four and five respectively. Finally concluding remarks are put forward in section six. In this chapter, the economic aspect of globalisation is being considered which is not to argue that the other dimensions are less important. They are not specifically addressed in this paper. Here globalisation is being taken in the sense of greater integration of the regional economy with the national economy and thus with the global economy. It involves the easier flow of capital, technology and goods and services across the borders, States and regions of a country.

Growth of Indian Industry during Reform Era

The development of any economy is always associated with some kind of structural transformation where the secondary and tertiary sectors are normally found to become relatively more and more important compared to primary sector. The changes in sectoral composition of GDP in India are shown in Table-13.1. In India the share of primary sector has gradually declined over the period after independence. The share of secondary sector during pre-globalisation era has increased from 15 per cent in 1950-51 to 29 per cent in 1990-91. During post liberalisation era the share of secondary sector has declined from 29 per cent in 1990-91 to 26 percent in 2003-2004. While the share of territory sector has increased from 29 per cent in 1950-51 to 40 per cent in 1990-91 (pre-globalisation era) and to 53 per cent in 2003-2004 (post- globalisation era). Thus it appears that the performance of the industrial sector after 1991 in terms of growth rate is not satisfactory.

The rates of growth in the index number of industrial production during the pre and post-globalisation period are depicted in table 13.2. It is evident from the table that the post liberalisation growth rates of industrial productions does not turn out to be better than the pre liberalisation growth rates as was expected. The average growth rate in manufacturing index during the period 1982-1990 was 6.8 per cent while during the period 1992-2000 it was 6.9 per cent only.

Table 13.1: Share of Different Sectors in GDP of India

Sectors	*1950-51*	*1970-71*	*1990-91*	*1998-99*	*2003-04*
Primary Sector	56	45	31	29	23
Secondary Sector	15	22	29	26	26
Territory Sector	29	33	40	45	53
Total GDP	100	100	100	100	100

Table- 13.2: Rate of Growth of Industrial Production (percent per annum)

Year	*Mining*	*Manufacturing*	*Electricity*	*General*
Average 1982-90				
1992-2000	*6.63.6*	*6.86.9*	*8.06.4*	*6.96.5*
1990-91	4.5	8.9	7.8	8.2
1991-92	0.6	-0.8	8.5	0.6
1992-93	0.6	2.2	5.0	2.3
1993-94	3.5	6.1	7.5	9.1
1994-95	9.8	9.1	8.5	13.1
1995-96	9.7	14.1	8.1	6.1
1996-97	-1.9	7.3	4.0	6.6
1997-98	6.9	6.7	6.6	4.1
1998-99	-0.8	4.4	6.4	6.6
1999-00	1.0	7.2	7.3	5.0
2000-01	3.6	5.3	4.0	6.9
2001-02*	1.8	2.8	4.6	2.9

Revised estimate.

Source: Central Statistical Organization

The average growth rates of industrial production on the basis of use-based classification are shown in Tables 13.3. It is evident from the table that a slowdown in capital goods sector and basic goods sector during post globalisation period. Growth in consumer goods and intermediate goods are also observed. This indicates a noteworthy change in the composition of manufacturing sector. This is of course due to the liberal import policy which has allowed imports of capital goods. The industrial growth in post reform era is mainly due to growth in production of consumer durable and intermediate goods. (Mahajan, 2004)

Table 13.3: Average Growth Rate of industrial Production

	1980-1991	*1992-2000*
Basic Goods	7.4	5.9
Capital Goods	9.4	5.4
Intermediate Goods	4.9	8.6
Consumer Goods	6.0	6.5
Consumer Durable	10.8	10.2
Consumer non-durable	5.3	4.7

Source: Indian Economic Survey Various Issue.

Table 13.4: Industrial Investment Proposals (Statewise)

Name of the State	*IEM+LOI+DIL*	
	Numbers	*Per cent*
1	2	3
Maharashtra	11007	19.57
Gujarat	6986	12.42
Tamil Nadu	5076	9.03
Uttar Pradesh	4837	8.60
Andhra Pradesh	3922	6.97
Haryana	3303	5.87

1	*2*	*3*
West Bengal	2944	5.24
Rajasthan	2639	4.69
Punjab	2434	4.33
Karnataka	2297	4.08
MadhyaPradesh	2180	3.88
Dadra and Nagar Haveli	1763	3.14
Chhattisgarh	866	1.54
Daman and Diu	799	1.42
Orissa	582	1.03
Pondicherry	581	1.03
Kerala	554	0.99
Goa	543	0.97
Himachal Pradesh	527	0.94
Delhi	501	0.89
Uttaranchal	490	0.87
Jharkhand	424	0.75
Assam	**292**	**0.52**
Jammu & Kashmir	209	0.37
Bihar	177	0.31
Meghalaya	**159**	**0.28**
Chandigarh	38	0.07
Tripura	**24**	**0.04**
Andaman and Nicobar	21	0.04
Sikkim	**14**	**0.02**
Nagaland	**13**	**0.02**
Lakshadweep	9	0.02
Manipur	**1**	**neg**
Mizoram	0	0.00
Location in more than one State	24	0.04
Total	**56236**	**100.00**

Note: IEM – Industrial Entrepreneur Memorandum, LOI – Letter of Intents, DIL – Direct Industrial Licences.

Source: SIA Statistics April 2004, Ministry of Commerce and Industry (GOI).

The growth of industry during post liberalisation era in India is not even. Increased industrial production has concentrated in industrially developed States. Thus they have consolidated their position more. Backward States like Uttaranchal, Jammu & Kashmir and North-Eastern States etc. are far behind in the race of industrialisation (Rana, *et al.* 2005)

The industrial investment proposals during the post globalisation period are shown in Table 13.4. It is evident from the table that the advanced States like Maharashtra, Gujarat, Tamil Nadu have further strengthened their position. The gap between the developed and backward States has further widened. It is surprising to note that around 20 per cent of the investment proposals received during the post-globalisation period are for a particular advanced State namely Maharashtra while all States of NER have a share of less than one per cent. Industrial growth of any State is however associated with actual flow of investments not with the number of proposals received. So far as actual flow of investments is concerned, the advanced States like Gujrat, Maharashtra, Tamil Nadu are much successful in attracting actual investment.

Industrial Entrepreneurs Memoranda implemented during 1992 to April 2004 is shown in Table 13.5. The top five States in terms of investments are Maharashtra, Gujarat, Tamil Nadu, Uttar Pradesh and Andhra Pradesh. The least States are Lakshadweep, Andaman & Nicobar, Tripura, Sikkim, Arunachal Predesh, Manipur, Mizoram and Nagaland.

Backward States continue to lag behind even in liberalised regime. Therefore, it appears that globalisation has hardly helped in boosting industrialisation in backward States. As the quantum of investment in these States is negligible, efforts must be made to develop an alternative model to boost the industrial development.

Table 13.5: Industrial Entrepreneurs Memoranda Implemented During 1992 April 2004

State/UTs	*Investment in Rs. Crore 1992-2004*	*% Share in Total 1992-2004*
Andhra Pradesh	438	7.95
Arunachal Predesh	0	
Assam	**51**	**0.92**
Bihar	6	0.10
Chattisgarh	52	0.94
Goa	86	1.55
Gujarat	971	17.61
Haryana	354	6.41
Himachal Prasesh	33	0.59
Jammu & Kashmnr	11	0.19
Jharkhand	36	0.65
Karnataka	159	2.88
Kerala	76	1.37
Madhya Pradesh	282	5.11
Maharashtra	870	15.78
Manipur	**0**	
Meghalaya	12	0.21
Mizoram	0	
Nagaland	0	
Orissa	35	0.63
Punjab	264	4.79
Rajasthan	333	6.03
Sikkim	**0**	
Tamil Nadu	405	7.34
Tripura	**4**	**0.07**
Uttaranchal	26	0.47
Uttar Pradesh	429	7.78
West Bengal	355	6.43
Andeman & Nicobar	0	
Chandigarh	4	0.07
Dadra & Nagar Haveli	69	1.25
Delhi	45	0.81
Pondicherry	40	0.72
Daman & Diu	69	1.25
Lakshadweep	0	
Total	**5515**	**100.00**

Source: Economic Times, 12 August, 2004.

Table 13.6: Industrial Investment Proposals (Sector-wise) (August 1991 March 2005)

SCHIND No andName	*IEM +LOI+ DIL*	
	Numbers	*Per cent*
1	2	3
Textile	8412	14.96
Metallukgical Industries	8205	14.59
Chemicals(Except Fertilizers)	7884	14.02
Misc Industry	5147	9.15
Electric Equipments	3303	5.87
Food Processing Industries	2842	5.05
Vegetable Oil and Vanaspati	2359	4.19
Drugs and Pharmaceuticals	2115	3.76
Sugar	1911	3.40
Paper And Pulp	1817	3.23
Misc Mech and Engg. Industries	1525	2.71
Industrial Machinery	1271	2.26
Telecommunications	1256	2.23
Cement and Gypsum	1170	2.08
Fermentation Industries	1056	1.88
Transportation	819	1.46
Prime Movers	707	1.26
Rubber Goods	605	1.08
Fertilizers	557	0.99
Fuels	453	0.81
Leather	401	0.71
Soaps, Cosmetics and Toiletries	397	0.71
Ceramics	392	0.70
Scientific Instruments	295	0.52

1	2	3
Commfoffice/Liouse	254	0.37
Glass	249	0.44
Machine Tools	202	0.36
Timber Products	146	0.26
Photographic Raw Film/Paper	123	0.22
Agricultural Machinery	82	0.15
Glue And Gelatin	59	0.10
Medical and Surgical Instr.	56	0.10
Dye Stuff	50	0.09
Industrial Instruments	42	0.07
Defence Industries	37	0.07
Boilers and Steam	26	0.05
Math. Survey	6	0.01
Drawing Instruments	5	0.01
Total	**56236**	**100.00**

Source: Economic & Political Weekly, May 20, 2004.

Sector-wise investment proposals are also shown in Table-13.6. It appears from the table that textiles, metallurgical and chemical industries have attracted nearly 40 per cent of the total investment in industry. Due to cheap labour and raw materials there sector has potential for rapid growth resulting industrial relocation.

Potential for Development of Industries in NE India

So far as industrialisation is concerned the region is yet to emerge out of industrial backwardness. This is reflected by the fact that the region's share in value added by manufacture is hardly two per cent with 3.02 per cent of existing SSI units. The process of setting up large and medium scale industries in the region is not satisfactory due to several constraints like undulating topography, lack of skilled and semi skilled manpower, limited size of market, inadequate infrastructure, limited financial resources of the State governments, insurgency and extremist problem, low level of per capita income and so on. In 1999 there are only 178 large & medium scale industries in NER. In the year 1993 the figure was only 166. Among the North-east States, Assam's share is 72.48 per cent (Table 13.7). The share of other States is negligible.

Small Scale Industry (SSI) thus, has been assigned a pivotal role in the scheme of industrialisation and economic development of the region. This can be witnessed in the developmental measures of both State and central government towards industrialisation in north-east region.

Table 13.7: Large and Medium Industries in North Eastern Region

Sl. No.	*Name of the State*	*No. of Units in 19931993*	*Percentage*	*No. of Units in 1999*	*Percentage 1999*
1	*2*	*3*	*4*	*5*	*6*
1	Arunachal Pradesh	17	5.8	17	9.55
2	Assam	118	74.8	129	72.48
3	Manipur	6	3.9	12	6.74
4	Meghalaya	7	4.5	10	5.62
5	Mizoram	1	0.3	1	0.56
6	Nagaland	16	10.4	7	3.93
7	Tripura	1	0.3	2	1.12
	Total	166	100.0	178	100.00

Source: Basic Statistics of NER, Various issues, NEC, Shillong.

The second and third all-India census of small scale industries were conducted in the year 1987-88 and 2001-02 respectively. These two censuses also reflect the post- and pre-globalisation scenario of SSI in India. A comparison of second

Table 13.8: Comparison of the Third Census with Second Census (Registered SSI Sector)

Sl. No.	*Indicator*	*2nd Census (1987-88) (pre-globalisation)*	*3rd Census 2001-02) (post-globalisation)*
1.	Percentage of Working Units	62.75	60.77
2.	Percentage of Working Units in rural areas	42.20	44.33
3	Percentage of Working Units that are		
	SSIs	96.24	65.55
	Ancillaries	0.52	5.08
	SSSBEs	3.24	34.45
4	Percentage of Proprietorship Working Units	80.48	88.85
5.	Percentage of Proprietorship Working Units engaged in Manufacturing/Assembly/ Processing	65.42	63.45
6.	Percentage of Working Units that are owned/Managed by SCs	6.84	7.85
	STs	1.70	3.53
	Women	7.69	8.32
7.	Per Working Unit Fixed Investment (Rs.Lakhs	1.60	6.68
8.	Per Working Unit Investment (Original) in P&M (Rs.lakhs)	0.95	2.21
9.	Per Working Unit production (Rs. Lakhs)	7.38	14.78
10.	Per Working Unit Employment (No)	6.29	4.48
11.	Employment per rupee one lakh of investment in Fixed Assets	3.94	0.67
12.	Production/Employment (Rs. Lakhs)	0.04	3.30

Source: Third All India Census of Small Scale Industries 2001-2002.

and third all-India census of small scale industries reveals the following facts. While the proportion of working units remained the same by and large, the domination of SSI among the working units has been reduced considerably from 96 per cent to 66 per cent. This is mainly due to the increase in the number of units engaged in services, as the number of units in manufacturing sector decreased only marginally from 65.42 per cent to 63.43 per cent. The per unit employment has also come down from 6.29 to 4.48. This could be due to technological up gradation and advancement being resorted to by the units in the Sector in the face of the changed economic competitive conditions. As a result, the per unit fixed investment has gone up from Rs. 1.60 lakh to 6.68 lakh. The comparison between the Second Census and in Third with respect to registered SSI sector in 12 identified indicators is presented in Table 13.8.

The total number of registered and unregistered SSI units in North-East India are shown in Table 13.9. It is estimated in

Table 13.9: Total SSI Sector in NER & India

Name of the State	*No. of Registered Units*	*No. of Un-Registered*	*Units Total*	*% in Total*
Arunachal Pradesh	255	997	1252	0.01
Assam	14,453	179,926	194,379	1.85
Nagaland	568	13,293	13,861	0.13
Manipur	4,599	43,400	47,999	0.46
Mizoram	2,733	8,383	11,116	0.11
Meghalaya	1,939	20,581	22,520	0.23
Sikkim	174	194	368	0.00
Tripura	959	23,393	24,352	0.23
Total of NER	25,450.5	290,167	315,847	3.02
Other State of India	13,49,523.5	88,56,049	102,05,343	96.98
India Total	**13,74,974**	**91,46,216**	**105,21,190**	**100.00**

Source : 3rd All India Census of Small Scale Industries 2001-2002, Ministry of Small Scale Industries, Govt. of India.

the 3rd census of SSIs, that the sector comprises 3,15,847 units spreading over the length and breath of north-east region. Assam has the highest number followed by Tripura and Manipur. The region's share in the country is 3.02 per cent. The nature of activities in the SSI sector of NER are also shown in Table-13.10. It can be observed from the table that except Arunachal Pradesh and Tripura all the States of North-East India have higher proportion of manufacturing units in comparison of national figure.

Table-13.10: Distribution of Total SSI units in NER by Nature of Activity (Percentage).

Name of the State	*Manufacturing*	*Repair & Maintenance*	*Service*	*Total*
Arunachal Pradesh	34.58	31.71	33.7	100.00
Assam	41.69	27.03	31.28	100.00
Nagaland	74.52	11.1	14.39	100.01
Manipur	65.74	14.14	20.12	100.00
Mizoram	49.57	2.72	47.72	100.01
Meghalaya	59.93	17.38	22.69	100.00
Sikkim	63.86	2.94	33.16	100.01
Tripura	25.2	17.83	34.40	100.00
All India	**39.69**	**16.36**	**43.95**	**100**

Source : 3rd All India Census of Small Scale Industries 2001-2002, Ministry of Small Scale Industries, Govt. of India.

In spite of various measures taken by the respective State governments, and Central government there has not been any significant improvement in the scenario. The National Council of Applied Economic Research (NCAER) made survey of industrial potential of the region. The team emphasized on forests and hydropower. North Eastern Industrial Consultants Ltd. (Report on Prospects and Possibilities of setting up Industrial estates in Manipur, Mizoram and Tripura,1995) and the respective State governments have also made the industrial survey potential of all the States in NER.

The natural resources, favourable agro-climatic conditions and traditionally skilful manpower available in the region reasonably advocates setting up of SSI units based on these resources and compatible with these conditions and circumstances (EDII,1992). The Shivaraman Committee suggested that in the north-eastern region, small scale industries based on locally available natural resources and industries capable of meeting growing local needs might be promoted. Considering the marketability and manpower ability, demand pattern and the existing constraints the most appropriate areas for small scale industries may be identified as follows : (i) forest based, (ii) agro based, (iii) livestock based, and (iv) Oil & gas based (v) mineral resources based and vi) service sector based. Therefore the respective State government and central government need to revamp its industrial policy and concentrate more on setting up industries based upon these. (Chakraborty, 2004)

NER is endowed with dense forests, occupying an area of about 11,688 hect. and accounting for more than 46 per cent of the total geographical area. Out of the total forest resources in the region only a small portion is in actual use, leaving large areas potentially exploitable. The forests are rich in timber, bamboo, cane, agar- wood, grasses and medicinal herbs. Thus the forests may provide raw materials to a number of small scale industries based on these resources. Considering the environmental aspects and sustainable development the forest can be utilized in a better way. The region can easily become a hub for medical plant based industries.

In natural rubber production, NER as a whole ranks second only to Kerala in the country. More and more plantations are reaching yielding stage and the productivity levels are also encouraging. In view of the area under plantations together with the growth potential and rubber production trends, the region has been identified as the second most rubber producing of the country. There is a vast potential for setting up of rubber-based industries in the region. The rubber produced in the region is also of high quality which faces trading problems in the absence of any rubber based industry in the region. In 2002-2003 an area of about 49,771 hectare land was under natural rubber plantation in the region. The raw rubber now produced is being sent out to the neighboring States for further value addition. This can easily be done in the State through development of rubber based SSI units.

Agriculture in the region can also play an important role in industrial development. It provides raw materials to a number of small scale and cottage industries. Cash crops and spices with commercial potentiality like sugarcane, jute, mesta, cotton etc. are being successfully cultivated in the region. Citronella, an aromatic crop has emerged as an important crop with industrial potentials. Production of essential oils from various species of herbs grown in the region may lead to development of industries like cosmetic, perfumery and pharmaceutical products. Production of high value, low volume items like pepin from papaya or pectin from citrus peel is pertinent for horticulture based SSI units in the State.

The agro-climatic conditions are favourable for growing various fruit and horticultural crops. The products of the region are well known- both in raw as well as processed form . There is scope for expansion of area under any specific variety, if required. Modern Food Processing Technology Park is also being set up in the region, to give a fillip to this sector. An Agri Export Zone for Pineapple is also being developed. There is a vast potential for setting up of food processing units in the region. Seasonal fruits such as pineapples, jackfruits, oranges, litchis etc. are grown in large quantities. The processed fruits can also be exported to Bangladesh. At present large quantities of fruits are informally traded with Bangladesh from NER. The marketable surplus of these is enough for opening up more fruit processing industries in the region as revealed by a study conducted by NEC.

Handloom and handicrafts are other potential areas for SSI units. At present handloom and handicraft is the largest industry in NER. There is wide scope to develop handloom industries in the small-scale sector. Cane and Bamboo handicrafts of NER are considered to be among the best in the country for the exquisite designs, wide range of products and artistic appeal. This industry has a great export potential as well. Steps have been taken to develop this industry on modern lines. Not only that, in view of availability of large bamboo resources in the region, industrial products like bamboo tiles, laminated products, ply, boards, corrugated sheets etc. can be produced, which can be used as building materials, for furniture manufacture etc. Studies have shown that bamboo is a very effective substitute for timber and is, in fact, better in many respects.

The region has immense reserves of gas which can generate power so essential for industrial, development. The natural gas reserves of the region have huge potentiality to generate power in excess of region's requirement. Recently, the North Eastern Electric Power Corporation (NEEPCO) and other organizations have initiated setting up of gas based power projects .If the target is achieved, NER will have a surplus in power generation .In the absence of any industrial base, NER can easily export the excess power to neighbouring countries.

Tourism is perhaps one of the most vibrant areas of economic development of the present times. Tourism can build transnational communities as people can interact with each other and develop a deeper sense of appreciation, cooperation and ultimately remove all narrow barriers and create new potential friendship between the two countries. NER is an attractive tourist destination. The region has a rich cultural heritage. The region also has rich flora and fauna. There is also great potential for development of tourist circuits if possible. All this offers attractive opportunities for the hospitality industry.. An attempt to relax visa rules, substituting passport entry by permit rules, encouraging package tours and allowing private tour operators will perhaps lead to open border system

The higher education that used to be considered as a public good is now increasingly being viewed as a private good. The efforts made by WTO legislating higher education as a private good , if implemented , then higher educational service would be treated like all other commodities and can be traded without much restriction . The higher education system in NER has deepened and widened over the period. Some significant changes have also taken place in higher education sector in tune with new economic policies. Privatization has already started shaping higher education system in NER. Private universities, technical and medical colleges are in the pipeline. .In view of above the region can explore the opportunity of providing higher education service to the students of neighbouring countries. At present very few students from the adjacent countries come to the region for higher education observing all visa formalities. The computer related programmes are much sought after by the learners.

Health care is another area where NER can explore the opportunity to provide service to neighbouring countries. It is a widely known fact that 20-30 per cent of indoor and outdoor patients of hospitals and private nursing homes in NER are residents of neighbouring countries. Most of them come illegally to this side of the border for better treatment. Relaxing visa rules or introducing permit system or even simply allowing them for a few days to consult doctors can legalize this service. People on both the sides of the border will be much benefited if this could be done.

Development Approaches

When one scrutinizes the policy stance of the Central government and the State governments of North East India towards industrial development of this region which can be classified industrially backward region, one finds two slightly different approaches. For the sake of convenience one can call them 'State Driven Industrial Development Model's (PDIDM) and 'Market Driven Industrial Development Model' (MDIDM). Of course, this is extremisation of the policy outlook of the government. But this way of looking at the approaches may bring certain critical issues of evolving a roadmap of industrial development of North East India into sharper focus.

One may first look at the Shukla Commission Report (1997) (SCR) from this analytical perspective. The major policy frame recommended by SCR can be summarized as follows:

SCR recommends that the thrust area for removing the roadblocks must be (a) Basic Minimum Services and (b) Infrastructure. Basic minimum services shall help in poverty alleviation. Infrastructure will facilitate economic development including industrial development. The responsibility of carrying this strategy forward will lie on local, State and central government. Planning Commission shall have the responsibility of determing the exact quantum of funding. Central assistance must have 90 per cent grant component. SCR argues that market forces are less likely to be effective in this region. Four deficits confront the North East: (a) basic needs deficit and, (b) infrastructure deficit, (c) resource deficit and, (d) a two way deficit of understanding with the rest of the country. SCR is careful enough to point out that this region cannot be treated a 'resource region' or 'market dumping region' or 'transit ward'. A feeling of participation is to be created through the policy interventions.

However, the same SCR also suggest other possibilities. It recognises that alternative roadmaps are possible. Special Economic Zones (SEZs) can be established to take advantage of the emerging opportunities of trade with Bangladesh and Myanmar. SCR encourages to place the development of North East India in several concentric circles :

a) local community

b) autonomous councils

c) States

d) region

e) larger world of South East Asia and South West China.

SCR also points out that the changing contours of economic policy may create possibility of inflow of private investment. However, in the face of uncertain security environment, it may become desirable for the government to underwrite critical investments with suitable counter guarantees.

Specifically, in the context of industrial sector SCR recommends the following :

a) The National Institute for Design, Ahmedabad should be invited to play a lead role for establishing design bureaus for textiles and crafts.

b) Special emporia and exhibition centres should be established in the region, in other parts of the country and abroad for promotion of marketing.

c) Proper areas should be selected like disputed areas along interstate boundaries for industrial activities with infrastructure support.

d) Special economic zones should be established in the North Eastern Region to attract export industries.

SCR is discussed in detail here because it is a comprehensive approach for outlining a road map of development for NER. We conclude from the tone of the report that it falls in the category of SDIDM.

The North-Eastern Council, Shillong has also come out with a document during the 10th plan period called "Road Map for Development of North Eastern Region" in two volumes. This is based on a brainstorming session with all the NE States held on 7-8-2003. The NEC document argues that the development strategy followed by the central and State governments have created an unbalanced economy in the North East India. The economics have remained based on agrarian sector. The industrial sector has mainly developed around tea, oil and timber (TOT) in Assam. Mining, saw mills and plywood factories are the major industries in the other North Eastern States. Even agriculture is undeveloped in this region. NER imports food items worth about Rs. 2000 to 2,500 crores annually. There is hardly any large or medium private industry outside Assam. Even within Assam, about fifty per cent of the industries are located in there districts namely— Kamrup, Tinsukia and Dibrugarh. If one looks at the value of output by manufacturing industries, one finds that industrial units are in food sector, wood and wood products, non-metallic and mineral products.

The main thrust of the NEC report seems to be trade-led development though it is not spelt out in so many words. The report recognizes that with a well thought out long term policy, the NER has the potential to emerge as a strategic base for domestic and foreign investors, to tap the potential of contiguous markets of China, Myanmar, Bangladesh, Laos, Thailand, Vietnam, Cambodia as well as Malaysia, Indonesia and beyond. The report quotes studies by India Institute of foreign Trade, which recommend that the whole North Eastern Region may be declared as Export Processing Zone.

Thus government policy stance as represented by SCR and NEC report has some thing to say on the role of trade- led growth and State supported growth.

But even these observations keep certain issues unclear. Traditionally, infrastructure is considered to be State domain and directly productive activities are mainly left to the private domain. However, today private public partnership (PPP) is considered to be essential even for the infrastructure sector. A more detailed analysis is necessary to see whether the PPP model shall be applicable for NER. Of special importance here will be the security perception of the private sector.

As far as, directly productive activities are concerned, here too specific analysis will be required to identify the industries where private initiative is likely to be of greater importance. As stated above, one of the objectives of this paper is to identify these industries. Relocation of industries in the sense of changing industrial composition of the region due to rapid growth of certain group of industries need to be guided by sequential and priority considerations.

Roadmap for growth of industry

Industrial development path of NER as impacted upon by market forces which mainly operate from the demand side and State interventions which mainly concentrate on supply side bottlenecks, like infrastructure, can be built into a State plus Market (S+M) led Industrial development path where TEN PIVOT POINTS can be identified.

From the perspective of removing *supply side bottlenecks* three issues become important.

Pivot point 1: Traditional development models have stressed on capital formation as a precondition for initiating the process of growth and development. Physical infrastructure is the most important component of the capital formation process.

Development of infrastructure, which includes power, transport communication and banking, has to be provided the highest priority. Due to backwardness of these region PPP model may not be effective for this region. State support is more critical here.

Pivot point 2: Development of Human Resources where vocational training and technology dissipation as well as entrepreneurship development have to be the key components for industrial development of this region. Various studies stand to confirm that there is abundance of natural resources in NER but due to lack of skilled manpower they are not properly harnessed (Das 2006, Chakraborty and Das 2006)

Pivot point 3: Development of special economic zones (SEZ) will take care of not only pivot points 1 and 2 but also aspects of tax benefit, subsidies and security environment. For industrial development leading to industrial relocation, not only supply side factors as discussed above are important but also the demand side factors have to be taken into consideration. The demand pull factors need to be given their due attention. These are discussed below :

Pivot point 4: One cannot ignore the insight of Adam Smith that division of labour (Industries) is limited by the size of the market. Domestic and external markets are, therefore, crucial generators of industrial activity. Encouraging trade led growth with linkages with markets of China, South East Asia, Bangladesh and Myanmar need to be accorded high priority.

The specific sectors where these forces of demand pull and supply support need to be concentrated based on comparative advantage of availability of locational specificities of natural resources on the one hand and traditional skills of the local people on the other hand can broadly be organised as the following pivot points.

Pivot point 5: Technological innovation and skill up gradation towards more value addition in primary sector activities like agriculture, pisci-culture, and vegetable production are required. One can look at the sectoral composition of GSDP of NER States to realize the potential of this sector.

Pivot point 6: Plantation sector like tea and rubber need to be similarly given an important pivotal role.

Pivot point 7: The NER has a rich heritage of Handloom industries. Commercial reorientation of Handloom sector is therefore required.

Pivot point 8: Commercial reorganization of Handicrafts sector also deserves due attention. It provides employment and is in harmony with traditional skills of this reason.

Pivot point 9: Development of industries based on gas and other mineral resources can be advocated due to large reserve of the resources as found in the States like Tripura.

Pivot point 10: Development of health care and eco tourism is justified on the ground that the NER has abundant natural resources and bio-diversity which can make the region an important destination of tourism in India. The region is still free from massive pollution of Air, Water and Soil.

The essence of the argument presented here is that strategies of accessing opportunities of globalisation shall have to be different for industrially backward regions of India. The assignment of role to public and private sector needs full consideration. The PPP model in infrastructure may not be suitable for NER of India.

This model of industrial development of NER can be shown in a flow chart:

CRUCIAL ROLE OF THE STATE→	1. INFRASTRUCTURE 2. HUMAN RESOURCE DEVELOPMENT ↓↑
	3. SPECIAL ECONOMIC ZONE ↓↑ 4. DIRECTLY PRODUCTIVE INDUSTRIAL ACTIVITIES ↓↑
CRUCIAL ROLE OF THE MARKET →	5. STRONGER NATIONAL AND WORLD MARKET LINKAGES

FLOW CHART OF 'S+M' LED DEVELOPMENT

If one looks at the model from the perspective of a road-map then the first milestones to be covered will be infrastructure and human resource development. The final destination will be total integration of NER economy with rest of India and then to the world economy. 'This S+M' led development path is feasible though the issues of sequencing of directly productive activities will necessarily be influenced by different random factors which cannot be predicted before hand.

Conclusion

The geographical location of North East India (NEI) has a special significance to international trade. The region share a longer border with neighbours like China, Bangladesh, Bhutan and Myanmar than mainland. Perhaps this is the reason why NEI should take interest in these countries for establishing international trade. NEI can take advantage of her close proximity to these countries by concentrating on export of industrial goods, apart from catering to the domestic market. The location of the region is also strategic in the international context, being between Bangladesh on one side and south East Asia on the other. In the past, the region had natural communication links – roads, rail and waterways – with and through these countries. Efforts are on for revival of these. If it happens, industrial relocation in the areas of rubber, tea, fruits processing, power, handloom and handicrafts, gas based industries, IT, tourisms and health care sector may occur within a short period.

It may also be mentioned here in the face of acute poverty and rising unemployment in the region the pressing need for rapid economic development has led the State governments to spell out their policies and programme in favour of industrialisation. In the process of achieving such rapid industrialisation, the growth of sickness in SSI units is causing a severe strain on the economic system of the region. The phenomenon of sickness not only tended to aggravate the problem of unemployment, but also rendered infractuous capital investment and consequently created an adverse climate for further industrial growth.

Various study groups and experts have identified the basic constraints for the development of SSI units. The strategy should therefore be framed to remove all such constraints. Any attempt in this respect may be viewed in a wider perspective involving all the States of NEI and central government, commercial banks, promotional organisations, financial institutions and entrepreneurs. As the region is endowed with abundant resources, entrepreneurs should be induced to set up industries based on these resources. For this, a detailed upto date inventory of available resources in the region will have to be made along with industry wise potential survey of all the States of NER. It is also necessary to have a data bank as a source of information accessible to entrepreneurs, which can guide them in decision making when selecting a new project or for expansion and diversification. (Chakraborty and Pramanik, 1999).

Note : NER and NEI are used in this chapter to denote the same region of India.

REFERENCES

Ahluwalia, Montek Singh (2001) : Economic Reforms –A Policy Agenda for the Future, *The Indian Journal of Commerce*, 54 (3), July-September, 2001.

Chakraborty, Kiran Sankar & Pramanik A.K. (1999), *Sickness in Small Scale Industries of North-Eastern Region*, Southern Economist, November 1.

Das, Gurudas (Ed.) (2005): *Structural Change and Strategy of Development – Resource Industry Linkages in North East India*, Akansha Publications, New Delhi.

Devadas, Rajammal P. (2001): Globalisation and Its Challenges for India in the 21st Century – An Introductionary note, *Bharatiya Samajik Chinton*, 24 (1-4), Dec.

Kumar, Arun (2004): Globalisation and India's Food Security : Issues and Challenges, Bharatiya Samajik Chinton, 2 (4), January.

Mahajan, Dhanashim (2004) : Performance of the Indian Industrial Sector, An Analysis, *Southern Economist*, 43 (10), September.

Mali, D.D. and Deka. P, (1987), *Industrial Development in North-East India*, Omson Publications, Guwahati.

Nagaiya, *Small Industry Development in India, Policy, Programmes and Institutional Support*, NISIET, Hyderabad.

North Eastern Council, *Toward Regional Development Plans and Perspective*, Publication No.8, Jan. 1980, Shillong.

North Eastern Industrial Consultants Ltd. (1995), *Report on Prospects and Possibilities of setting up Industrial Estates in Manipur*, Nagaland, Mizoram and Tripura for IDBI, Agartala.

Rana, Kondle and Gupta (2005) : Indian Industry in the Era of Reforms, *The Indian Journal of Commerce*, 58, (3), July-September, IP 185-203.

14

Economic Inequality in Pre- and Post-Reform Periods in India with Focus on the Northeastern Region

Introduction

Planning Commission, Government of India, in its document "Towards Faster and more Inclusive Growth: An Approach to the 11th Five-year Plan (2006)" states that: divides and disparities at present of our country has at least four aspects: socio-economic deprivations of backward communities, gender gap, rural-urban divide and regional inequality." Regional inequality has again inter-regional and intra-regional dimensions. 'Inequality', itself is a value-laden term (Sen, 1975) having connotations which are not only economic but social, cultural and political. The 'Approach Paper' further observes in the specific context of regional economic inequality that balanced regional development has been an important objective of development planning in India. In the pre-reform period various instruments including fiscal incentives, industrial policies and directly targeted programmes have been deployed for this purpose. However, in the post-reform period since 1991, some of the earlier instruments such as industrial licensing are no longer available. Investments will now flow to different regions based on infrastructure and attractive investment climate. However, different analysis carried out on regional inequality in the periods centering around 1991 show that regional economic inequality is on the rise (Ahluwalia, 2002; Bhattacharya and Shaktivel, 2004). However, the studies have ignored experiences of Northeast on the ground that reliable and sufficient data are not available for these States. Sikkim is a new entry in the Northeast policy frame. Mizoram does not report SDP data at constant prices. Yet, a broader analysis of regional economic inequality including the other Northeastern States is possible and desirable. One of the major objectives of this chapter is to carry out this analysis. This chapter also presents the emerging pattern of inequality within the States of Northeast in pre and post-reform period. An attempt is also made to derive policy implications for the central and State governments from these findings.

The chapter is divided into five sections including this section where the perspective and objectives of the chapter are indicated. Section II deals with some methodological issues regarding measurement of economic inequality. Section III explains the database of the chapter including their limitations. Section IV presents the findings. Section V concludes with a discussion of policy implications of the findings for central and State governments.

METHODOLOGY OF THE STUDY

Sen (1975) discusses certain basic methodological issues in conceptualisation and measurement of economic inequality, which are of relevance for the present chapter to avoid certain pitfalls of analysis and interpretation. Economic inequality is a concept, which cannot avoid an interface of 'normative' and 'objective' aspects. From the perspective of the analysis presented in this dissertation, the normative aspects are contoured by the policy perspectives of the society and the government as articulated in plan document like the 'Approach Paper' to the 11th Plan. The objective aspects of measurement, however, deserve more attention. Sen considers five' objective, measures of income inequality: (i) range, (ii) relative mean deviation, (iii) co-efficient of variation, (iv) standard deviation of logarithms and (v) gini co-efficient. Each measure interprets income inequality in different ways. A little amount of thinking shows that the range and gini co-efficient have conceptually mathematical underpinning but measures based on dispersion have conceptually a statistical nuance. A statistician looks at the numbers as outcomes of data generating mechanism where the numbers have frequency distribution. This distribution can be defined in terms of four aspects: central tendency, dispersion, skewness and kurtosis. This 'dispersion' has a kind of natural base. If dispersions are taken as measures of inequality then certain amount of inequality is inherent in the world of the statistician. From the perspective of the statistician, therefore, dispersions can indicate 'rising' or 'falling' inequality in terms of at least two modes of approach. One is to see whether income distribution follows 'normal' distribution taking the 'chi-squared test' of goodness of fit. The other is to investigate whether the variances differ over space, time or control-experimental groups. This is F-test approach based analysis of variance. This chapter does not aspire to attain this level of statistical sophistication. Only the trend of co-efficient of variation over time period under study is considered. In the context of the present study, 'pre-reform period' is 1980-81 to 1990-91 and post-reform period is 1991-92 to 2003-04.

There is another dimension of information, which is not captured by the co-efficient of variation, which is case-specificity. If the average per capita NSDP remains the same and State A which is 10 units above the average and State B which is 10 units below the average change their position with B taking the place of A and A taking the place of B, then co-efficient of variation will remain the same though this information has lot of economic significance. Ranking of the States over the period may be observed to investigate whether the pattern of inequality is undergoing any significant change in the period under consideration. This numerical exercise is combined with the statistical approach based on co-efficient of variation to study pre and post-reform regional inequality in India in general and Northeastern Region in particular.

DATA SOURCE

The difficulties of estimation of State Domestic Product (SDP) in India are well documented (EPW Research Foundation, 2003). For the commodity producing sectors, SDPs are estimated on the basis of 'income method' based on estimates of value added per worker. Here two major problems are faced. One is absence of data for the current or reference period. The other is the presence of large 'unorganised' sector for which estimates of value added per worker is rather scarce. Any in-depth discussion of these problems is beyond the scope of the present chapter.

Database of the present investigation is shown in the following Table 14.1.

Table 14.1: Data Source

Type [at constant (1993-94) prices]	*Year*	*Data Source*
Per Capita NSDP	1980-81	EPWRF
	1985-86	EPWRF
	1990-91	EPWRF
	1995-96	EPWRF
	2000-01	CSO
	2003-04	CSO
Growth Rate of GSDP	1980-81 to 1992-93	EPWRF
	1993-94 to 2003-04	CSO

For other types of data used in this chapter, references are made at the related tables.

Reforms, Growth and Inequality

Focus on Northeastern Region of India

One may begin with a few theoretical speculations. Let there be two regions in an economy – A and B. A is advanced. B is backward. Let the per capita income of A be Rs.100. Let it be Rs. 50 for B. The gap in per capita income is of course Rs. 50. Both regions experience a growth rate of 6.9 percent per year so that in 10 years they double their per capita income. Per capita income of A is Rs.200 and that of B is Rs.100. The gap has also doubled to Rs.100. If both regions experience similar growth rate of population, which is zero or a constant then the same conclusion, may be drawn from analysis of growth rate of total income also. GDP growth rate and per capita growth rate will tell the same story. It is obvious that per capita income gap between the two regions can be reduced only if the region B grows at a faster rate than A. If region B is experiencing a higher population growth then this growth rate has to be so much faster.

This line of reasoning has empirical implications. Coefficient of variation may be calculated for 14 so-called 'major' States on the basis of growth rate of GSDP. Now, growth rates of Northeastern States of India are added and the co-efficient of variation is again calculated. If the new inclusions are clustered around the arithmetic mean then co-efficient of variation after inclusion shall in fact *decline*. This means that the growth rates of these Northeastern States are not significantly higher or lower than the average. But to reduce the gap in per capita NSDP, higher rates are required. Since this has not happened so the co-efficient of variation of per capita NSDP will, in fact, *increase*. If this trend is observed as one moves from pre-reform to post-reform period then one can say that post-reform has not been particularly benign for the States in the Northeast of India.

If this much of the argument put forward here is granted then one can extend the analysis in at least four different ways. One can study the pattern of intra-regional inequality. One can look at the sectoral composition of NSDP of these States. One can look at the infrastructure situation of these States. Similarly one can look at the Human Development index.

However, it must be recognised that the convergence-divergence debated in post-reform India can accommodate the experience of the Northeastern States and they do have important policy implications.

But what could be the possible objections to the line of argument presented here?

First, as EPW Research Foundation (2003) points out, change in the time periods tends to effect the trend of co-efficient of variation in significant ways. Since the dividing line between pre and post-reform period remains subjective in various ways, therefore, conclusions drawn on trend on co-efficient of variation are tentative to a large extent. It may be clearly recognised that the problem is not so much with the argument as its empirical verification. Reforms began in 1991, but economic agents might have taken sometime to realise the full implication of the policy shift, then again some more time in taking relevant decision and then finally implement those decisions. Thus the year from which reforms had impact on the economy has to be identified more carefully. If this cannot be done then it is perhaps safer to note the growth rates of different States but avoid any attempt in determination of either rising or declining regional economic inequality.

Second, the growth rate of SDPs of different States is influenced by domestic policy environment, seasonal factors like monsoons, performance in exports from different States etc. Thus the behaviour of growth rates and their pattern in post-reform period cannot be attributed to reforms alone. However, one can investigate the performance of different States in post-reform period when economic policy regime has gone through a sea change and is creating a new macroeconomic environment without suggesting that the growth rates are outcomes of economic reforms alone. As a result the emerging patterns of inequality cannot be attributed to policy stance of 1991 alone.

Third, growth rate of GSDP may deviate over the short run from the natural rate of growth. Thus, short period upward movement of growth rate may not indicate a structural break in the long-run natural rate of growth. Sufficiently long time series of four or five decades may be necessary to draw inferences with greater degree of confidence.

Fourth, as the Kuznets conjecture on the relationship between growth and inequality argues, growth may have different type of impact in the short period and in the long run. Therefore, the inequality patterns need to be studied in a rather descriptive mode without attempting to draw conclusions beyond the given data set in a particular time period.

The analysis presented should be interpreted in the context of observations made above.

Growth Rate of GSDP

A scrutiny of Table 14.2 shows that average growth rate of GSDP at 1993-94 prices for 19 States (consisting of 14 States considered by Ahluwalia and five Northeastern States, namely, Assam, Arunachal Pradesh, Manipur, Meghalaya and Tripura) has declined from 5.30 per cent per year in pre-reform period to 5.14 per cent in post-reform period.

For comparable periods but taking all States EPWRF estimates are 5.26 percent and 5.82 per cent respectively. Non-inclusion of Goa and Pondicherry may have effected the results. Pondicherry grew at 10.09 percent and Goa at 8.38 percent in post-reform period. Another factor might have been extension of the period of analysis upto 2003-04. However, co-efficient of variation shows an increase for 16 major States in the case EPWRF. A similar increase is found for the 19 States considered here. If one takes the Northeastern States exclusively the average growth rate of the States is slightly higher at 5.65 percent and 5.43 per cent for pre and post-reform periods respectively. But there is a decline in average growth rate, which is in harmony with 19 State averages situation. The co-efficient of variation is higher in the post-reform period for the Northeastern States. The standard deviation in fact increased considerably from 1.73 per cent to 2.17 per cent.

Table 14.2: Growth Rate of GSDP of 14 States and Northeastern States

(at 1993-94 prices)

States	*1980-81 to 1990-91*	*1991-92 to 2003-04*
1. Bihar	4.66	0.82
2. Rajasthan	6.6	5.84
3. Uttar Pradesh	4.95	3.43
4. Orissa	4.29	4.12
5. Madhya Pradesh	4.56	2.61
6. Andhra Pradesh	5.65	5.81
7. Tamil Nadu	5.38	5.61
8. Kerala	3.57	5.74
9. Karnataka	5.29	6.93
10. West Bengal	4.71	6.94
11. Gujarat	5.08	6.82
12. Haryana	6.43	5.72
13. Maharashtra	6.02	5.82
14. Punjab	5.32	4.40
15. Assam	3.58	2.92
16. Arunachal Pradesh	8.34	4.29
17. Manipur	5.06	4.92
18. Meghalaya	5.51	6.41
19. Tripura	5.76	8.60
For 19 States		
Mean	5.30	5.14
Standard deviation (s.d.)	1.10	1.83
Coefficient of Variation (C.V.)	0.21	0.36
For first 14 States		
Mean	5.18	5.04
s.d.	0.83	1.78
C.V.	0.16	0.35
For NE States		
Mean	5.65	5.43
s.d.	1.73	2.17
C.V.	0.31	0.40

Source: EPWRF and CSO.

Per Capita NSDP

Per capita NSDP of the 14 States considered by Ahluwalia and 7 Northeastern States except Mizoram are considered in Table 14.3. In 1980-81, per capita NSDP of most of the States were within the range Rs.3000 to Rs.8000. But in 2003-04, only 4 States remained at this level – Bihar, Uttar Pradesh, Orissa, Madhya Pradesh, Assam and Manipur. Rajasthan is no more in this category. Thus the word BIMARU may be now changed by the word M (Manipur), U (Uttar Pradesh), M(Madhya Pradesh), B (Bihar), A (Assam) and O (Orissa), i.e., MUMBAO, though such lexicographic orderings may not be the real concern of economic analysis.

Table 14.3: Per Capita NSDP of 14 States and Northeastern States at Constant (1993-94) Prices

(in Rs.)

Year States	*1980-81*	*1985-86*	*1990-91*	*1995-96*	*2000-01*	*2003-04*
1. Bihar	3427	4014	4474	2728	3831	3396
2. Rajasthan	4254	4657	6760	7216	8175	10010
3. Uttar Pradesh	4133	4446	5342	5229	5575	5975
4. Orissa	4085	4483	4300	5053	5549	6640
5. Madhya Pradesh	5084	5275	6350	6778	7195	8149
6. Andhra Pradesh	4604	5248	6873	8086	10195	11756
7. Tamil Nadu	5266	6321	7864	10177	12994	12976
8. Kerala	5692	5688	6851	8748	10714	12328
9. Karnataka	4943	5347	6631	8368	11854	12634
10. West Bengal	4952	5387	5991	7492	9796	11608
11. Gujarat	6455	7274	8788	11649	12489	16302
12. Haryana	7514	9172	11125	11570	13848	15752
13. Maharashtra	7102	7890	10159	13221	14233	16765
14. Punjab	8442	10257	11776	13008	15071	16119
15. Assam	4636	5451	5574	5760	5943	6466
16. Arunachal Pradesh	4017	5418	6927	9424	9153	10253
17. Manipur	4400	4955	5395	5612	6851	7532
18. Meghalaya	5441	5645	6928	7221	9476	10795
19. Nagaland	5726	6954	8313	9646	11473	NA
20. Tripura	4001	3795	5026	5707	9397	11136
21. Sikkim	NA	NA	NA	7633	10119	12026
For 21 States						

1	*2*	*3*	*4*	*5*	*6*	*7*
Mean	5208.7	5883.85	7072.35	8110.762	9711	10930.9
s.d.	1304.83	1674.846	2077.154	2752.843	3117.969	3732.931
C.V.	0.251	0.285	0.294	0.339	0.321	0.342
For first 14 States						
Mean	5425.21	6104.21	7377.43	8523.07	10108.50	11457.86
s.d.	1454.71	1876.67	2317.93	3119.83	3574.58	4184.83
C.V.	0.268	0.307	0.314	0.366	0.354	0.365
For NE States						
Mean	4703.50	5369.67	6360.50	7286.14	8916.00	9701.33
s.d.	728.13	1024.34	1247.95	1726.73	1901.30	2197.10
C.V.	0.155	0.191	0.196	0.237	0.213	0.227

Source: Same as Table 2.

If per capita NSDP of 21 States are considered then the co-efficient of variation shows a rising trend from 0.25 in 1980-81 to 0.34 in 2003-04. The same trend is noticed if the 14 major States are considered. However, the co-efficient of variation is higher. This can be explained on the basis of the fact that the per capita NSDP of other Northeastern State than Assam and Manipur are nearer to the average per capita NSDP of the States which was around Rs.11000 in 2003-04.

Though there are some missing observations for Sikkim and one for Nagaland, but it cannot be denied that inequality in per capita NSDP exists within the Northeastern region. The post-reform period has seen certain amount increase in this inequality due to low level of performance of Manipur and Assam and rapid rise in per capita NSDP in Tripura, Meghalaya and Sikkim.

Ranking Northeastern States on Per Capita NSDP

The rank of a State in terms of per capita NSDP improves if it experiences a growth rate of per capita NSDP which is higher than that of others. In 1980-81, the rank of Tripura was

6th among the Northeastern States excluding Mizoram and Sikkim. As Table 14.4 shows in 2000-01 it has improved its position to the 3rd rank. On the other hand, rank of Assam had declined from 3rd to 6th in the same period as shown in Table 4. Nagaland has maintained 1st rank throughout this period. Meghalaya has remained at the second rank but for the year 1995-96 when it had 3rd rank. Manipur had declined from 4th rank to 5th rank. Arunachal Pradesh had improved its rank from 5th to 4th.

Table 14.4Rank on Per Capita NSDP of North-Eastern States

States	*Rank*				
	1980-81	*1985-86*	*1990-91*	*1995-96*	*2000-01*
Assam	3	3	4	4	6
Arunachal Pradesh	5	4	3	2	4
Manipur	4	5	5	6	5
Meghalaya	2	2	2	3	2
Nagaland	1	1	1	1	1
Tripura	6	6	6	5	3

Source: Same as Table 2.

Sectoral Composition of NSDP of Northeastern States

It has been noted above that among the Northeastern States Assam has failed to attain a higher growth rate of GSDP. Manipur has also recorded a slightly lower growth rate in post-reform years. However, Tripura has attained a higher growth rate in post-reform years. Table 14.5 presents the sectoral composition of NSDP of 5 Northeastern States.

The higher growth rate attained in Tripura is due to service sector. In 2000-01, it had 55 percent share in the NSDP. Meghalaya also has a large tertiary sector which was around 55 percent of NSDP in 2000-01. In contrast, tertiary sector's share has

Table 14.5: Sectoral Composition of NSDP at Constant (1980-81 and 1993-94) Prices

States	*Sector*	*1980-81**	*1985-86**	*1990-91**	*1995-96®*	*2000-01®*
Assam	Primary	48.07	46.55	44.41	46.73	44.57
	Secondary	11.54	12.10	11.23	13.47	15.17
	Tertiary	40.39	41.35	44.36	39.8	40.26
Arunachal Pradesh	Primary	47.28	52.93	46.19	41.88	37.84
	Secondary	22.21	19.9	21.56	29	20.12
	Tertiary	30.51	27.17	32.25	29.11	42.04
Manipur	Primary	49.11	43.78	38.02	35.68	30.32
	Secondary	7.65	9.04	10.20	16.56	21.14
	Tertiary	43.25	47.18	51.78	47.76	48.55
Meghalaya	Primary	41.88	39.22	35.14	33.73	32.59
	Secondary	14.55	11.93	10.65	10.99	12.26
	Tertiary	43.56	48.85	54.21	55.28	55.15
Tripura	Primary	55.92	50.87	43.88	35.77	29.73
	Secondary	7.56	4.48	5.46	10.08	15.34
	Tertiary	36.51	44.65	50.67	54.15	54.93

Note: * at 1980-81 prices ® at 1993-94 prices

Source: Same as Table 2.

remained almost constant in Assam in the period 1980-81 to 2000-01 at around 40 percent. In fact, primary sector had a larger share of around 45 percent in Assam in 2000-01. Arunachal Pradesh presents a slightly different picture. The secondary sector has been dominantly present from the year 1980-81 and this share has remained more or less stable with marginal gain of the tertiary sector and decline of primary sector. The point to note is that Northeastern States are undergoing structural change with considerable diversity in this change. Ofcourse, a more detailed break-up of the three sectors is necessary to understand the nature of change of the economies of Northeastern States.

CONCLUSIONS AND POLICY PRESCRIPTIONS

The major conclusions, which can be drawn from the analysis presented above are as follows:

Like rest of India, Northeastern States have experienced a deceleration of growth rate of GSDP from 5.65 percent per year to 5.43 percent per year.

Out of the 5 Northeastern States considered in the present study, only Tripura and Meghalaya have experienced a higher growth rate than All-India average of 19 States. Assam grew only a 2.92 percent per year (compound annual growth rate estimated from log linear function) which is almost half of the All-India average of 19 States.

Regional inequality as measured by co-efficient of variation of per capita NSDP has increased in Northeastern region in the span of years 1980-81 to 2003-04. This result includes Nagaland and Sikkim but excludes Mizoram due to non-availability of estimates at constant prices for this State.

Sectoral change or composition of NSDP in terms of primary, secondary and tertiary sectors is not uniform for the States of Northeast India. Assam shows signs of structural stagnation. In Meghalaya and Tripura, tertiary sector has taken up a dominant position.

Ranks of the States in terms of per capita NSDP again support the proposition that Assam has not generated high growth. It is now at the bottom rank (2000-01). Nagaland has however retained its number 1 rank over the pre and post-reform period.

From the conclusions drawn from this study, certain policy implications follow. In the post-reform era, those States will be able to grow faster which can attract domestic and foreign investment. The Approach Chapter to the 11th Plan suggests that this flow of investment is crucially dependent on physical infrastructure, human resource and a healthy investment climate.

If infrastructure alone were important then the performance of Assam will be difficult to explain. Rank of States of Northeast India obtained from different Finance Commission estimates is presented in Table 14.6. In the year 2000, Assam ranked 2nd.

But as Table 14.7 shows, in 1991 Assam ranked 5th among the States in terms of Human Development index. Manipur held the 1st rank and Tripura 3rd. Better health and education of the people may also contribute to generation of basic capabilities. Therefore, it seems logical to argue that for the country in general and Northeastern States in particular infrastructure and human resource development have to be the thrust areas of policy intervention of Central and State governments.

Table 14.6: Rank on Infrastructure of Northeastern States

States	*1995*	*Rank*	*2000*	*Rank*
Assam	82	2	53.84	2
Arunachal Pradesh	49	6	32.08	6
Manipur	70	5	37.29	5
Meghalaya	74	3	46.88	4
Nagaland	71	4	51.02	3
Tripura	84	1	54.6	1

Source: North Eastern Council, 2003.

Table 14.7: Rank on Human Development Index of Northeastern States

States	*1981*	*Rank*	*1991*	*Rank*
Assam	0.272	5	0.348	5
Arunachal Pradesh	0.242	6	0.328	6
Manipur	0.461	1	0.536	1
Meghalaya	0.317	3	0.365	4
Nagaland	0.328	2	0.486	2
Tripura	0.287	4	0.389	3

Source: NHDR 2001.

REFERENCES

Ahluwalia, Montek Singh (2002) "Economic Performance of the States in the Post Reforms Period" in *Indian Economy Since Independence* (ed.) Uma Kapila, 14th Edition, Academic Foundation, Delhi.

Bhattacharya and Shaktivel, 2004 "Regional Growth and Disparity in India: A Comparison of Pre and Post-reform Decades" *EPW*, Vol. 39, No. 10, March 6, 2006.

CSO, downloaded from internet.

Economic and Political Weekly Research Foundation (2003) "*Domestic Product of States of India 1960-61 to 2000-01*", June.

North Eastern Council, Government of India (2003) "*Road Map for Development of North Eastern Region*", Vol. I and II, Shillong.

Planning Commission, Government of India (2002) "*National Human Development Report 2001*", Oxford University Press, New Delhi.

Planning Commission, Government of India (2006) "*Towards Faster and More Inclusive Growth: An Approach to the 11th Five Year Plan*", June 14, 2006 (downloaded from internet).

Sen, Amartya (1975) "*On Economic Inequality*", Oxford University Press, Delhi.

15

Primary Education in North-east India in the Era of Sarva Shiksha Abhiyan

Introduction

The National Policy on Education, 1986 and 1992 declared the goal of Universalisation of Elementary Education (UEE). Education for children of the age group 6-14 years has been made a fundamental right by the 86th constitutional amendment. This directive of State policy is the result of cumulative effort social activists, research by eminent social scientists, articulation of the felt need of the people by the political forces and pressure from pan-national organisations like the United Nations. Theoretical foundation of the spread of primary education as a means and goal of development has been constructed by Amartya Sen, Jean Dreze (1995) and others. It cannot be denied that there have been various attempts at improvement of primary education in India prior to 2001 when Sarva Shiksha Abhiyan (SSA) was launched. Some examples are: Area Intensive Education Project (AIEP) for Human Resource Development, Primary Education Curriculum Renewal (PECR), Developmental Activities in Community Education and Participation (DACEP), Comprehensive Access to Primary Education (CAPE) in the seventies and eighties and more recently the Andhra Pradesh Primary Education Programme (APPEP), Bihar Education Project (BEP), Lok Jumbish and District Primary Education Programme (DPEP). Centrally sponsored schemes such as mid-day meals, Operation Blackboard, Teacher Education Improvement, Non-

Formal Education etc. were also launched to maximise the efforts in this direction. On the basis of the lessons learnt from the implementation of these programmes and keeping in view the needs of different regions of the country which were not covered by the earlier programmes, Sarva Shiksha Abhiyan was launched in the year 2001. The programme is for all children of India in the age group 6-14 years wherever they may live, whatever their caste, community, creed and gender. Therefore, it is the largest programme in primary education not only in India but also in the whole world.

The SSA has a clear time frame expressing the political will of the country to give her children quality basic education to promote social justice effectively involving Panchayati Raj Institutions, Tribal Autonomous District Council, State Governments and the Central Government providing an opportunity for having own visions at the local level converging all earlier programmes and other government programmes of poverty alleviation and promotion of quality of life.

A close look into the indicators of primary education in North Eastern States reveals that there are areas where policy-makers' intervention are urgently required and above all, there are significant variations among the States. At the same time it is also found that the literacy rate in general and particularly female literacy rate in most of the north eastern States are much higher than the national average. These unique features of primary education in north eastern States of India require further analysis. The national effort at improving the primary education situation of the country has important implication for the North-east India. It is recognized that evolution of primary education from its traditional, local and even parochial roots all over the country to a broader platform of national interaction can only further integrate the primary education system of North-east India to other parts of the country. This convergence is likely to take place for all regions of the country. Yet, the study of this region in the context of primary education has remained underreported. One of the goals of this paper is to remove this lacuna. The paper has four sections including the present one where the theme of the paper is introduced. Objective, data source and method of analysis are discussed in section two. Section three deals with the findings of the paper. While summary and conclusion are put forward at the end in section four.

Objective of the paper

The objective of the present paper is to analyse the status of primary education in north eastern States of India by making a comparative study of the performance of the States. The performances of primary education in selected States are assessed in terms of the following indicators.

i) School related indicators,

ii) School facility indicators,

iii) Teacher related indicators,

iv) Enrolment related indicators, and

v) Performance of students related indicators.

Data Source

The basic database of the analysis is the data released by National Institute of Educational Planning and Administration based on District Information of School Education (DISE) of 2005. There are eight States in the north-eastern region, Assam, Arunachal Pradesh, Meghalaya, Mizoram, Manipur, Nagaland, Sikkim, and Tripura. However, due to lack of data Manipur and Arunachal Pradesh are not considered in this analysis.

There are certain limitations of DISE data, which may be pointed out here. Firstly, during 2005 data were collected for 1.04 million schools and 4.17 million teachers but the coverage of schools have varied from State to State in the case of schools like Navadaya Vidyalayas, Kendriya Vidyalayas, Sainik Schools, Open Schools etc. Secondly, a few schools have not responded to all the classificatory variables like year of establishment, school category, sex code of teachers, etc. A few school did not report age and grade matrix so that estimation of GER and NER become difficult. Reporting of school age population has remained incomplete, which is necessary for GER and NER. The analysis presented here should be judged in the context of these limitations of data.

Method of Analysis

To reduce data overload some techniques of preparing composite indicators have to be employed.

Factor analysis has been popular in designing weighting diagram for construction of composite indicators. Irma Adelman and Cynthia M.Taff (1971) observes that the primary purpose of factor analysis is to reduce the original number of explanatory variables to a smaller number of independent "factors" in terms of which the whole set of variables can be understood. We start by taking the simple correlation coefficients of the k numbers of indicators. These correlation coefficients may be arranged in a table, which is called the correlation table. The elements of the diagonal would be unity as they are the self-correlated, i.e., the correlation of each Xi with itself (r xi, xi = 1 for all the i's). The correlation matrix is symmetrical, i.e., the elements of each row are identical to the elements of the corresponding columns, since rxi xj = rxj xi.

Sum of each column (or row) of the correlation table is computed, obtaining k number of sums of simple correlation coefficient. Σkirxi xj= Σkirxi xj We compute the sum total of the column (or row) sums-ΣkiΣkjrxi xj and we take its square roots.Finally, we obtain the factor loadings for the first Principal Component P1by dividing each column (or row) sum by the square root of the grand total. aij= (Σkirxi xj) / (□□□√□□ΣkiΣkirxi xj) It should be clear that the loading thus obtained are the correlation coefficients of the respective indicator with the composite index

First Principal Component is constructed in the following way:

$$P_1 = a_{11} x_1 + \alpha_{12} x_2 + \ldots + a_1 kxk$$

The sum of the squares of the loading of the Principal Component is called the latent root (or Eigenvalue) of this component and is denoted by the Greek letter λ with the subscript of the Principal Component to which it refers. The importance of the latent root or the eigen value lies in the fact that it expresses the percentage of variation in the set of indicators the Principal Component explains. The loadings in our study have been tested based on the levels of significance of the Pearson Correlation coefficients. In this particular exercise, multi-stage Principal Component Analysis of selected variables is carried out. Within a sub-group, the indicators have a high degree of inter-correlation, while the canonical correlation between pairs of sub-groups is low on an average. The Principal Component Analysis has then been applied to each of these 5 sub-groups of variables. The first Principal Components obtained from different sub-groups have been treated as a set of new variables and combined at a second stage to obtain the Final Composite Index. It has been argued that this method overcomes the necessity of taking more than one Principal Component in the analysis, since the correlation among the variables in a subgroup are generally high and consequently, the first Principal Component explains an 'adequate' proportion of the variation in the data matrix. However, the results are almost similar in both the procedure followed in this study which are discussed in the section where the results are analysed. The relative performance of the States in SSA can be assessed by ranking the States in terms of school related, school facility based, teacher related, enrolment related and student performance related indicators which represent the factors of analysis and captured in terms of a composite index of these indicators.

Analysis and Findings

The analysis based on the five sub-groups indicated above may be considered as under.

School related indicators

The following school related indicators are considered here:

a) Percentage of schools established after 1994 of total number of schools in the State;
b) Percentage of schools with pucca building in 2005;
c) Average number of classrooms per school in government and private management;
d) Percentage of good condition classrooms schools;
e) Student-Classroom Ratio (SCR);
f) Percentage of single classroom school in government and private management; and
g) Percentage of single teacher school in 2004-05.

One may argue that if SSA is successful then there will be more schools established after 1994 because SSA mandate is that there should be a primary school within one kilometer for each habitation. In this case Sikkim has the first rank, Tripura has the second rank and Assam has the sixth rank as shown in Table 15.1. The all India percentage is 25.15. This means that out of four schools one school has been established after 1994.For Sikkim, Tripura and Meghalaya the percentage is higher than the all India percentage.

The SSA is supposed to increase percentage of schools with pucca building. If one ranks the States in terms of this indicator Assam has first rank, Tripura has second rank and Mizoram has the sixth rank. This is below the national figure of 71 percentage as shown in Table 15.1.

Successful implementation of SSA would lead to increase in number of class-rooms. Here Nagaland holds the first rank, second rank is held by Mizoram and Sikkim. Assam has the lowest rank. For Mizoram, Nagaland, Sikkim and Tripura average number of class-room is higher than the national average of 2.4 classrooms per school In the case of percentage of good conditions classrooms schools Sikkim has the first rank, Tripura has the second rank and Nagaland has the sixth rank. In all cases the percentage is lower than the all India level .Student-Classroom Ratio should be low but too low a ratio is not also desirable. In all northeastern States SCR is low compared to the national average of 45 student per class. Only in case of Assam the

Table 15.1: School Related Indicators

States	Indicators									
	X1	X2	X3	X4	X5	X6	X7	X8	X9	X10
Assam	30477	0.76	42.21	1.5	1.9	25.90	59	66.51	45.39	23.01
Meghalaya	6356	25.41	22.38	2.0	2.5	24.81	22	28.91	25.79	15.26
Mizoram	1318	18.82	10.17	3.9	4.4	30.25	19	2.33	0.88	5.61
Nagaland	1523	12.15	12.02	4.9	5.3	20.43	17	0.15	0.65	4.60
Sikkim	732	30.19	26.41	3.9	4.9	52.11	12	0.72	0.00	1.37
Tripura	1785	25.77	33.56	3.0	6.2	47.73	29	17.77	0.00	0.06
All India	**693030**	**25.15**	**71.18**	**2.4**	**4.9**	**63.36**	**45**	**15.55**	**4.88**	**18.15**

Source: *Elementary Education in India, Progress towards UEE*, Analytical Report 2004-05, Arun C. Mehta.

Note: X1—Number of schools, X2—Percentage of schools established after 1994 of total number of schools in the state, X3— Percentage of schools with *pucca* building in 2005, X4—Average number of classrooms per school in government management, X5—Average number of classrooms per school in private management, X6—Percentage of good condition classrooms schools, X7—Student-Classroom Ratio (SCR), X8—Percentage of single classroom school in government management, X9—Percentage of single classroom school in private management, X10—Percentage of single teacher school in 2004-05.

number is large at 59 students . It is obvious that with progress of SSA percentage of single classroom should fall. Here Nagaland has the first rank, Sikkim has the second rank and Assam has the sixth rank. In fact in case of Assam the percentage of single teacher school is as high as 66 percent which is more than four times the national figure .SSA should reduce the percentage of single teacher school. Here Tripura has the lowest percentage and therefore the highest rank. The rank of Assam is sixth.

The composite index has been constructed to assess the overall situation of school related indicators. Here the indicators considered are: (i) Percentage of schools established after 1994 of total number of schools in the State; (ii) Average number of classrooms per school in government management; (iii) Percentage of good condition classrooms schools; and (iv) The inverse of Student-Classroom Ratio because of positive pair wise correlation. The weights assigned to them are 0.28, 0.22, 0.22, and 0.28.

From the composite index one finds that Sikkim has the first rank, Tripura has the second rank and Assam has the sixth rank. This will imply that SSA has been implemented better in the sphere of creation of schools in Sikkim followed by Tripura, Meghalaya, Mizoram, Nagaland and Assam (Table 15.2)

TABLE 15.2: Composite Index of School Related Indicators

States	*C1*	*Rank*
Assam	6.19	6
Meghalaya	12.98	3
Mizoram	12.74	4
Nagaland	8.95	5
Sikkim	20.7	1
Tripura	18.3	2

Note: C1—Composite index of school related indicators, C2—Composite index of school facility indicators,C3—Composite index of enrolment indicators, C4- Composite index of performance indicators

School Facility Indicators

The following indicators are considered here. (a) Percentage of schools having drinking water facility; (b) Percentage of schools having blackboard at ground level; (c) Percentage of schools without blackboard; (d) Percentage of schools having computer; and (e) Percentage of schools having playground.

If SSA is effective in a State then percentage of schools having drinking water facility will be high. In this case Sikkim has first rank, Mizoram has second rank and Meghalaya has the sixth rank. In all cases the percentage is lower than the All –India level, which is 78.8 percent as shown in Table 15.3.

Table 15.3: Schools Facility Indicators

	Indicators				
States	*X1*	*X2*	*X3*	*X4*	*X5*
Assam	62.62	19.08	4.61	1.61	45.08
Meghalaya	37.08	20.55	18.66	1.45	24.75
Mizoram	62.75	19.04	8.12	1.67	10.09
Nagaland	38.48	68.29	27.77	3.47	36.38
Sikkim	73.63	64.89	21.45	12.43	39.21
Tripura	57.59	47.68	6.05	1.57	51.60
All India	78.80	48.78	7.07	4.50	44.92

Source: Elementary Education in India, Progress towards UEE, Analytical Report 2004-05, Arun C. Mehta

Note: — X1—percentage of schools having drinking water facility, X2—percentage of schools having blackboard at ground level, X3—percentage of schools without blackboard, X4—percentage of schools having computer, X5—percentage of schools having playground.

With progress of SSA, percentage of schools having blackboard at ground level will be high. Here, Nagaland has the first rank, Sikkim has the second rank and Assam has the sixth rank. The all India percentage is 48.78. For Nagaland and Sikkim the percentage is higher than the all India percentage.

SSA should reduce the percentage of schools without blackboard. Here Assam has the lowest percentage and therefore the highest rank.The rank of Tripura is second and Nagaland has the sixth rank. If SST is effective then the percentage of schools having computers should increase. In terms of this indicator Sikkim has the first rank, Nagaland has the second rank and Meghalaya has the sixth rank.

Percentage of schools having playground should be high. Here Tripura has the first rank, Assam has the second rank and Mizoram has the sixth rank. Only for Tripura and Assam the percentage is higher than the All-India percentage of 44.92 (Table 15.3).

Overall situation of facility in schools can be studied using composite index. The indicators considered are: i) Percentage of schools having drinking water facility; ii) Percentage of schools having blackboard at ground level; iii) Inverse of the percentage of schools without blackboard; iv) Percentage of schools having computers.

The weights assigned to them are 0.20, 0.29, 0.31and 0.20 respectively based on principle component analysis which generates the eigen vector. Sikkim has the first rank, Tripura second rank and Meghalaya last rank in terms of composite index. This is shown in Table 15.4.

Table 15.4: Composite Index of School Facilities

	Indicators	
States	*C2*	*Ranks*
Assam	27.56	4
Meghalaya	18.72	6
Mizoram	20.49	5
Nagaland	35.64	3
Sikkim	45.03	1
Tripura	36.05	2

III) *Teacher Related Indicators*

The following teacher related indicators are considered here: a) Average number of teacher per school in government and private management, and b) Pupil-Teacher Ratio (PTR).

The average number of teacher per school should be higher in government managed schools if SSA is effective. Here Nagaland and Sikkim hold first rank, Mizoram and Tripura have the second rank and Meghalaya last rank.For Assam, average number of teacher per school is same as the All-India average of 3 teachers per school but for Mizoram, Nagaland, Sikkim and Tripura, it is higher than the All-India average (Table 15.5). Pupil-Teacher ratio should be low. In all considered northeastern States it is low compared to the all India level of 42 pupil per teacher. Among the northeastern States PTR of Assam is high, which is 34 pupil per teacher and PTR of Sikkim is low which is 10 pupil per teacher.

Table 15.5: Teacher Related Indicators

	Indicators		
States	*X1*	*X2*	*X3*
Assam	3	2	34
Meghalaya	2	3	20
Mizoram	4	5	20
Nagaland	5	6	15
Sikkim	5	5	10
Tripura	4	7	23
All-India	3	5	42

Source: Elementary Education in India, Progress towards UEE, Analytical Report 2004-05, Arun C. Mehta

Note: X1—Average number of teacher per school in government management, X2—Average number of teacher per school in private management, X3—Pupil-Teacher Ratio.

Table 15.5 shows that except for Assam, average number of teachers is higher in private schools compared to government managed schools. It is interesting to note that the number of students per teacher is highest in Assam compare to other States. Therefore Pupil Teacher Ratio alone captures most of the information about sufficiency of teachers in primary schools. Hence the States are ranked on the basis of PTR alone. Here Sikkim secures the 1st rank and not very surprising Assam has the lowest rank(Table 15.6).

TABLE 15.6: Index of Inverse of the Pupil Teacher Ratio

	Indicators	
States	*C3*	*Rank*
Assam	0.03	6
Meghalaya	0.05	3.5
Mizoram	0.05	3.5
Nagaland	0.07	2
Sikkim	0.10	1
Tripura	**0.04**	**5**

Enrolment Related Indicators

Enrolment related indicators are: (a) Percentage of enrolment in government schools to total enrolment; (b) Gender Parity Index (GPI) in all areas and in rural areas; (c) Gross Enrolment Ratio (GER); and d) Net Enrolment Ratio (NER).

All these indicators will have high values with the progress of SSA. If one ranks the States in terms of enrolment in government schools then Assam has the first rank, Tripura second rank and Meghalaya sixth rank. Only for Assam, Tripura, and Meghalaya the percentage is higher then the All-India level of 85.03 percent. (Table 15.6) In terms of GPI, Meghalaya has the first rank, Sikkim second rank and Tripura sixth rank . For Tripura the value of this index is same as the All-India index of 0.91.SSA is supposed to increase GER. In the case of GER Mizoram holds the first rank, Sikkim second and Tripura third. In the case of NER, among the six northeastern States Tripura has the first rank, Mizoram second and Nagaland sixth.

Table 15.7: Enrolment Related Indicators

	Indicators				
States	*X1*	*X2*	*X3*	*X4*	*X5*
Assam	97.54	0.96	0.96	99.92	87.78
Meghalaya	62.51	1.01	1.02	127.56	94.64
Mizoram	92.55	0.94	0.94	157.91	117.89
Nagaland	79.67	0.95	0.94	115.16	97.52
Sikkim	81.49	0.98	0.98	143.19	86.94
Tripura	97.53	0.91	0.9	138.29	121.8
Kerala	35.51	0.97	NA	76.44	64.12
Bihar	99.63	0.78	NA	91.05	81.97
All-India	85.03	0.91	0.9	NA	NA

Source: Elementary Education in India, Progress towards UEE, Analytical Report 2004-05, Arun C. Mehta

Note: X1—Percentage of enrolment in government schools to total schools, X2— Gender Parity Index (GPI) in all areas, X3—Gender Parity Index (GPI)rura l areas X4— Gross Enrolment Ratio (GER), X5— Net Enrolment Ratio (NER).

Overall situation of enrolment related indicators could be assessed form the composite index. Here the indicators considered are: (i) Percentage of enrolment in government schools to total enrolment; (ii) Gross Enrolment Ratio; (iii) Net Enrolment Ratio.

They have positive pair wise correlation. The weight assign to them are 0.25,0.34 and 0.41.From the composite index one finds Mizoram has the first rank, Tripura second and Sikkim third (Table 15.8).

Table 15.8: Composite Index of Enrolment Related Indicators

	Indicators	
States	*C4*	*Rank*
Assam	94.3	6
Meghalaya	97.84	5
Mizoram	125.17	1
Nagaland	99.08	4
Sikkim	104.63	3
Tripura	121.38	2

Performance Related Indicators

The considered performance related indicators are: a) Average flow rate (I-V) consists of Promotion, Repetition and Dropout and b) Input per graduate (years).

With the progress of SSA promotion rate should be increased. In this case Mizoram has the first rank, Nagaland second and Sikkim has the sixth rank. For Kerala and Bihar the rates are 91.0 percent and 78.6 percent (Table 15.7). Repetition rate should fall. Here Mizoram has the lowest repetition rate and therefore it has the first rank. Assam second rank and Sikkim sixth rank. In all considered northeastern States repetition rate is higher than Kerala which is 3.2 percent. The repetition rate of Bihar is 13.7 percent. Dropout rate will be low. For Mizoram it is lower and therefore it has the first rank. Nagaland second rank and Assam sixth rank. Dropout rate of all the northeastern States is lower than Kerala (5.8) and Bihar (7.7). Input per graduate will be low for each State if SSA is effective. For Meghalaya and Mizoram it is lower and thus they hold the first rank. Second rank is held by Nagaland and Sikkim has the lowest rank. For Assam, Meghalaya, Mizoram and Nagaland input per graduate is lower than Kerala of 8.7 years whereas for Bihar it is 11.3 years.

Table 15.9: Performance Related Indicators

	Indicators			
States	*X1*	*X2*	*X3*	*X4*
Assam	91.8	4	4.2	8.3
Meghalaya	85.0	11.8	3.2	5.9
Mizoram	98.2	3.7	-1.9	5.9
Nagaland	94.3	7.2	-1.5	7.5
Sikkim	72.6	25.2	2.2	14.0
Tripura	76.2	22.1	1.6	13.2
Kerala	91.0	3.2	5.8	8.7
Bihar	78.6	13.7	7.7	11.3

Source: *Elementary Education in India, Progress towards UEE, Analytical Report 2004-05,* Arun C. Mehta

Note: X1— Promotion, X2— Repetition, X3— Dropout, and X4— Input per graduate (years).

Table 15.10: Composite Index of Students' Performance Related Indicators

	Indicators	
States	*C5*	*Rank*
Assam	32.95	3
Meghalaya	30.48	4
Mizoram	35.25	1
Nagaland	33.81	2
Sikkim	26.00	6
Tripura	27.30	5

Overall situation of performance related indicators can be assessed by the composite index. Here indicators considered are: (i) Promotion rate; (ii) Inverse of the repetition rate;

(iii) Inverse of the input per graduate because they have positive pair wise correlation. The weights assign to them are 0.36,0.33 and 0.31. From the composite index one finds Mizoram has the first rank, Nagaland second and Sikkim has the sixth rank. (Table 15.10)

Overall Performance of Six Northeastern States

Overall performance of the six northeastern States can be assessed from the average value of the composite index of school indicators, school facility indicators, enrolment indicators, performance indicators and the inverse of the pupil-teacher ratio. From this average value one finds that Tripura has the first rank, Sikkim second and Meghalaya sixth. This will imply that SSA has been implemented better in Tripura followed by Sikkim, Mizoram, Nagaland, Assam and Meghalaya. (Table 15.11)

Table 15.11: Overall Performance of the Six Northeastern States

States	*C1*	*C2*	*C3*	*C4*	*C5*	*Average value*	*Rank*
Assam	6.19	27.56	94.3	32.95	0.03	32.21	5
Meghalaya	12.98	18.72	97.84	30.48	0.05	32.01	6
Mizoram	12.74	20.49	125.17	35.25	0.05	38.74	3
Nagaland	8.95	35.64	99.08	33.81	0.07	35.51	4
Sikkim	20.7	45.03	104.63	26.00	0.10	39.29	2
Tripura	18.3	36.05	121.38	27.30	0.04	40.61	1

Note: C1—Composite index of school related indicators, C2— Composite index of school facility indicators,C3— Composite index of enrolment indicators, C4- Composite index of performance indicators, C5— Inverse of the pupil-teache ratio.

Summary and Conclusion

The following points have emerged from the above analysis:

1) The composite index of school related indicators reveals that Sikkim has the first rank, Tripura has the second rank and Assam has the sixth rank. This will imply that SSA

has been implemented better in the sphere of creation of schools in Sikkim followed by Tripura, Meghalaya, Mizoram, Nagaland and Assam.

2) Sikkim has the first rank, Tripura second rank and Meghalaya last rank in terms of composite index of school facility related indicators.

3) In all northeastern States PTR is low compared to the all India level of 42 pupil per teacher.

4) The average number of teacher per school should be higher in government managed schools if SSA is effective. Here Nagaland and Sikkim hold first rank, Mizoram and Tripura have the second rank and Meghalaya last rank.

5) The composite index of enrolment related indicators shows that Mizoram has the first rank, Tripura second and Sikkim third.

6) The composite index of performance related indicators shows that Mizoram has the first rank, Nagaland second and Sikkim has the sixth rank.

7) In terms of overall performance of the five sub-group indicators ,it seems SSA has been implemented better in Tripura followed by Sikkim, Mizoram, Nagaland, Assam and Meghalaya

This chapter aims to identify the strengths and weaknesses of the States of NER in the field of primary education. This kind of analysis may help the policy makers in decision making and for better monitoring of the affairs of primary education. From the analysis presented above, one finds that the performance of the States of Northeast India differs when different groups of indicators are considered. Therefore, in a sense it is difficult to describe a particular State a good performer in terms of school related indicators, school facility related indicators, teacher related indicators, enrolment related indicators and performance of the student related indicators. However, if one attempt to construct composite indicators and a simple average of these indicators are taken then a particular ranking pattern emerges where Tripura attains the first rank and Meghalaya attains the last rank. However, the purpose of the exercise is not merely ranking the States in terms of these indicators but to identify areas of strength and weaknesses in different aspects of SSA. These may have useful policy implications as well. Better monitoring and evaluations and ensuring a more participatory delivery mechanism may go long way in improving the performance of the Northeastern States in the field of primary education.

REFERENCES

Adelman, Irma and Cynthia M.Taff (1971); Analysis of Variance Technique for the Study of Economic Development.*Journal of Development Studies, VIII, Oct., 93-94*

Das, Amarendra (2007): How Far Have We Come in Sarva Siksha Abhiyan? *Economic and Political Weekly January 6* .

Government of India: *Economic Survey –2005-06,* Ministry of Finance, Economic Division.

Jean, Dre'ze and Amartya Sen (1995): *INDIA –Economic Development and Social Opportunity,* Oxford University Press, Delhi.

Mehta, Arun C (2006): *State Report Cards 2005, Elementary Education in India: Where Do We Stand?* National Institute of Educational Planning and Administration, Department of Elementary Education and Literacy, Ministry of Human Resource Development, Government of India, New Delhi.

Bibliography

Adelman, Irma and Cynthia M.Taff (1971); Analysis of Variance Technique for the Study of Economic Development.*Journal of Development Studies, VIII, Oct.*

Agarwal, A.K. (1988) : *North Eastern Economy : Problems and Prospects,* Mittal Publications, New Delhi.

Ahluwalia, Montek Singh (2001) : Economic Reforms –A Policy Agenda for the Future, *The Indian Journal of Commerce,* 54 (3), July-September, 2001.

Bangladesh-India Chamber of Commerce and Industries (2000): *India Bangladesh Infrastructure Summit,* December 21, 2000, Calcutta.

Bhattacharjee, P.R. (1993): *Economic Transition in Tripura,* Vikash Publishing, New Delhi.

Bhattacharya and Shaktivel, 2004 "Regional Growth and Disparity in India: A Comparison of Pre and Post-reform Decades" *EPW,* Vol. 39, No. 10, March 6, 2006.

Bhattacharya, Jayanta (2001): *Tripura–Bangla: From History to Future,* paper presented at the third dialogue on interaction with Indian Bordering States, organized by the Bangladesh Institute of International and Strategic Studies, Dhaka, August 21-23, 2001.

Bhattacharya, Pallab: *Indo-Bangla Trade, PTI Feature.* (www.sentinelassam.com/sentinel_en/archives/aug1704/editorial.htm)

Bhende, Asha A. Kanitkar, Tara (2001): *Principles of Population Studies,* Himalaya Publishing House, Mumbai.

Bonner (1992): Total Quality Education, *Public Administration Review*, September -October.

British Standards Institutions (1991): *Quality Vocabulary* Part-2, London.

Chakraborty, D. (2004) : *Land Question in Tripura*, Akansha Publishing House, New Delhi.

Chakraborty, K.S. (1997): TQM Concept in Higher Education of India, *Vidyasagar University Journal of Commerce*, Vol.2, March.

Chakraborty, K.S. (2005): 'Structural Change and Strategy of Development Resource – Industry linkage in Tripura', in *Structural Change and Strategy of Development*, ed. by Gurudas Das, Akansha Publishing House, New Delhi.

Chakraborty, K.S. and Haldar, P.K. (1998) : Re-engineering Higher Education in India, Business Studies, Department of Commerce, Calcutta University, Vol. XXI, July.

Chakraborty, Kiran Sankar (2002): Sickness in Small Scale Industries of Tripura, *Vidyasagar University Journal of Commerce*, vol.7, Midnapur.

Chakraborty, Kiran Sankar (2004): Structural Change and Strategy of Development – Resource-Industry Linkages in Tripura, in '*Structural change and strategy of development*', Gurudas Das (ed.), Akansha Publications, New Delhi.

Chakraborty, Kiran Sankar & Pramanik A.K. (1999), *Sickness in Small Scale Industries of North-Eastern Region*, Southern Economist, November 1.

Chakraborty, Kiran Sankar and Das, B.C. (2002): An inside into the development of SSI in Tripura, *Southern Economist*, 41, (8), Bangalore.

Chaterjee, Achintya (1994): Quality Excellence or Extinction, *The Indian Journal of Commerce*, Vol. XVIII, Part-3, No. 180, Sept.

Chowdhury, N.R.(1996): *Higher Education Delivery Systems- Trying the TQM Option,* University News, Sep.

Cox, Peter R (1970): *Demography,* Cambridge.

Crawford and Shutler (1999): Total Quality Management in Education, problems and issues for classroom teachers, *The International Journal of Educational Management.*

Crosby (1979): Quality is free: Art of Marking Quality Certain, McGraw Hill,

Dahiya, L.N. (2004): India's International Trade in Higher Education, *Indian Journal of Commerce,* 57, (3).

Das, Amarendra (2007): How Far Have We Come in Sarva Siksha Abhiyan? *Economic and Political Weekly January 6* .

Das, B.C. (2004): Health Care Facilities in Tripura, paper presented in the national seminar organized by the Department of Economics, Tripura University and ESSOT, Agartala on 18th –19th September 2004 at Agartala.

Das, Gangadhar(2004):fruits and Vegetables Production in North Eastern Region: Export potential, *The Indian Journal of Commerce,* 57, (3).

Das, Gurudas (Ed.) (2005): *Structural Change and Strategy of Development – Resource Industry Linkages in North East India,* Akansha Publications, New Delhi.

Deb Burman S.B.K. *A study over the Jhum and Jhumia Rehabilitation in the Union Territory of Tripura,* Government of Tripura, Agartala, 1971.

Deming (1986): *Out of the Crisis,* Cambridge University Press.

Devadas, Rajammal P. (2001): Globalisation and Its Challenges for India in the 21st Century – An Introductionary note, *Bharatiya Samajik Chinton,* 24 (1-4), Dec.

Directorate of Statistics,Government of Tripura; *Some Basic Statistics of Tripura* (Various issues)

Economic and Political Weekly Research Foundation (2003) *"Domestic Product of States of India 1960-61 to 2000-01"*, June.

Entrepreneurship Development Institute of India (1992): *Project Opportunities in Tripura*, Gujarat.

Gibbs, Jack P. (1960) *Urban Research Methods*, Affiliated East - West.

Gilmore (1974): *Product Conformance Cost*, Quality Progress.

Government of India, Census of India - Various Issues.

Government of India, Census Reports, Various Issues.

Government of India: *Economic Survey –2005-06*, Ministry of Finance, Economic Division.

Government of Tripura (2000): Speech of Minister, Industries and Commerce, Government of Tripura in 'First National Conference of Small Scale Industries,' Vigyan Bhavan, New Delhi 30th August, 2000.

Government of Tripura, (2002): Education Department, *Higher Education Scenario of Tripura.*

Government of Tripura, Department of Industries and Commerce (2004): *Tripura The Land of Opportunities*, Agartala.

Government of Tripura, Department of Industries and Commerce (2002): Speech of Chief Minister, Tripura, in the seminar on 'Promotion of Trade and Investment Between Tripura and Bangladesh', 31st May 2002.

Government of Tripura, Directorate of Economics and Statistics, *Statistical Abstract*, Various Issues.

Government of Tripura, Directorate of Economics and Statistics: *Statistical Abstract*, Various Issues.

Government of Tripura, Directorate of Industries: *The Second All India Census of Registered Small Scale Industries.*

Government of Tripura, Directorate of Industries: *Tripura Incentive Scheme*, 1995.

Government of Tripura, Evaluation Organisation (1975): *Evaluation Report on Industrial Estates in Tripura.*

Government of Tripura, Tripura Industrial Development Corporation (1998-99): Industrial Potential Survey in Tripura Prepared by TCS.

Government of Tripura, Tripura Industrial Development Corporation (2001): *Investment Opportunities and Industrial Infrastructure in Tripura.*

Hans Raj (1999): *Fundamentals of Demography*, Surjeet Publications.

Hansen and Jackson (1996): TQM in the classroom, Quality in Higher Education.

ICAR: *Human Nutrition vis-à-vis Animal Nutrition in India.*

ICMR Advisory Committee (1981): *Recommended Dietary Intakes for Indians*, Indian Council for Medical Research, New Delhi.

Jalil Altaf (2004): Northeast India-Bangladesh Initiatives Map, Bangladesh Enterprise Institute, Dhaka.

Jean, Dre'ze and Amartya Sen (1995): *INDIA –Economic Development and Social Opportunity*, Oxford University Press, Delhi.

Juran (1988): *Quality Control Handbook*, McGraw Hill, New York.

Khasnobis and Nath (1994): Urban growth and Urbanisation in West Bengal, Business Studies, C.U. Vol. XXII.

Krishnamurthy, J. (1984): Changes in the Indian workforce, *EPW*, Vol. XIX, No. 50.

Kumar, Arun (2004): Globalisation and India's Food Security : Issues and Challenges, Bharatiya Samajik Chinton, 2 (4), January.

Land Acquisition Department – No. 2509 – 10/DM/LA/SS/60/54 dt. 4th March, 1957. (Tripura Secretariat Archives)

Mahajan, Dhanashim (2004) : Performance of the Indian Industrial Sector, An Analysis, *Southern Economist*, 43 (10), September.

Mali, D.D. and Deka, P. (1987): *Industrial Development in North-East India*, Omson Publications, Guwahati.

Mishra, B.D (1995): *An Introduction to the Study of Population*, South Asian Publishers Pvt. Ltd, New Delhi.

Mitra, Ashok (1980): *Population and Area of Cities and Town and Urban Agglomerations*, 1872-1971, Allied, Calcutta.

Motwani and Lumar (1997) The need for implementing *TQM* in Education, *lntemation Joumal of Educational Management*.

Mukhapadhyay (2000) *Management of Quality in Higher Education, University News.*

Nagaiya, *Small Industry Development in India, Policy, Programmes and Institutional Support*, NISIET, Hyderabad.

Nathan, Keyfitz (1977): *Applied Mathematical Demography*, John Wiley and Sons, New York.

National Assessment and Accreditation Council (2002): *NAAC A Profile*, Bangalore.

National Council of Applied Economic Research (1961): *Techno Economic Survey of Tripura*, New Delhi.

North Eastern Council, Government of India (2003) "*Road Map for Development of North Eastern Region*", Vol. I and II, Shillong.

North Eastern Council, *Toward Regional Development Plans and Perspective*, Publication No.8, Jan. 1980, Shillong.

North Eastern Council: *Basic Statistics of North Eastern Region*, 2004, Shillong.

North Eastern Council: *Toward Regional Development Plans and Perspective,* Publication No. 8, Jan. 1980, Shillong.

North Eastern Industrial Consultants Ltd. (1995), *Report on Prospects and Possibilities of setting up Industrial Estates in Manipur,* Nagaland, Mizoram and Tripura for IDBI, Agartala.

Planning Commission, Government of India (2002) *"National Human Development Report 2001"*, Oxford University Press, New Delhi.

Planning Commission, Government of India (2006) *"Towards Faster and More Inclusive Growth: An Approach to the 11th Five Year Plan"*, June 14, 2006 (downloaded from internet).

Pollard, A.H ; Yusuf, Farhar; and Polland, G.N (1981); *Demographic Techniques,* Pergamon Press.

Ramkrishnan, Venkitesh (2008): *Hope and Fear, Frontline,* Feb 29, 2008.

Rana, Kondle and Gupta (2005) : Indian Industry in the Era of Reforms, *The Indian Journal of Commerce,* 58, (3), July-September.

Sallis(1996): *TQM in Education,* London, Kogan Page.

Sen, Amartya (1975) *"On Economic Inequality"*, Oxford University Press, Delhi.

Sherr and Lozier (1991): *TQM in Higher Education,* San Francisco.

Srivastava, O.S (1998): *Demography and Population Studies,* Vikas Publishing House Pvt. Ltd.

Subramanyam, K. (1996): 'Total Quality Management in Higher Studies', *The Hindu,* June, Madras, p. 26.

Swaminathan, M (1997): Essentials of Food and Nutrition, Val-11. The Bangalore Printing and Publishing Co. Ltd, Bangalore United Nations (1996): *World Population Assessment and Projection.*

Tripura University: *Annual Report* (2002-2003).

United Bank of India (1970): *Report of the Fact-finding Survey of Tripura,* Calcutta.

Verghese, B.G. (2002): Tripura eyes Bangladesh, *The Statesman,* 22th June 2002.

Visaria, Pravin (1991): "India Population: Emerging perspective of the 1991 Census", *Demography-India,* Vol. 20.

Index

❑❑❑